200,000 HEROES

Italian Partisans and the American O.S.S. in WW II

Leon Weckstein

HELLGATE PRESS   ASHLAND, OREGON

200,000 HEROES

©2011 Leon Weckstein

Published by Hellgate Press

(An imprint of L&R Publishing, LLC)

Hellgate Press
PO Box 3531
Ashland, OR 97520
www.hellgatepress.com

Editing: Harley B. Patrick
Cover design: L. Redding

Library of Congress Cataloging-in-Publication Data

Weckstein, Leon, 1921-
200,000 heroes : Italian partisans and American O.S.S. in WW II / Leon Weckstein. -- 1st ed.
    p. cm.
Includes bibliographical references.
ISBN 978-1-55571-698-1
1. World War, 1939-1945--Underground movements--Italy. 2. World War, 1939-1945--Campaigns-
-Italy. 3. Guerrillas--Italy--History--20th century. 4. Guerrillas--Italy--Biography. 5. United States.
Office of Strategic Services--History. 6. Weckstein, Leon, 1921- 7. World War, 1939-1945--Personal
narratives, American. 8. Soldiers--United States--Biography. 9. United States. Army--Biography. 10.
United States. Army. Infantry Division, 91st--History. I. Title. II. Title: Two hundred thousand heroes.
D802.I8W425 2011
940.54'8645--dc23

                              2011031936

Printed and bound in the United States of America
First edition 10 9 8 7 6 5 4 3 2

Italian partisans worked with increasing boldness behind German lines. Armed with weapons captured from Germans or dropped by Allied aircraft, they were often trained and organized by Allied officers who penetrated enemy lines or parachuted behind them. Sensing that the time was ripe for action, partisan bands stepped up their activity, cutting telephone wires, ambushing troops and dynamiting culverts, bridges, roads and railroad tracks.

And all across northern Italy the partisans rose up. On a signal, railway workers sabotaged track in a number of provinces to prevent the movement of German troops and supplies. In Genoa partisan groups cut off water and electricity service to German barracks and established roadblocks to prevent enemy troops from escaping, or being reinforced. In a pitched battle they thwarted German demolition squads bent on destroying the city's port installations. Their ranks swelled with overnight volunteers...guerilla brigades in dozens of other Italian cities, including Milan and Turin...forced the surrender of German garrisons and were firmly in control by the time the Allied troops arrived.

(Excerpted from the renowned Time-Life World War II book titled, *The Italian Campaign*, written by Robert Wallace and editors of that series.)

"Seen any signs of partisan activity?"

A Bill Mauldin cartoon from 1944 depicting three German soldiers desperately trying to evade any Partisans that might be near. Though in France at the time, Mauldin humorously illustrates the fear the enemy had developed regarding the Italian Partisans. Leon Weckstein visited the two-time Pulitzer Prize-winning cartoonist two weeks before he passed away in 2003 to present him with a Medallion for Excellence from the 91st Infantry's leader, General Rodney Kobayashi.

CONTENTS

The author (*center*) with Partisans Emmio Sardelli (*left*) and Riccardo Barchielli (*right*). Florence, Italy, 2000.

AUTHOR'S NOTE

Epic actions of the Italian and American heroes that follow are not fiction. Their truth resides in historic files, biographical field reports and Partisan recollections that remain vividly galvanized within their aging, yet canny minds.

With such helpful details and with Partisan urging, their soul-stirring stories ached to be revived into a compact chronology for all to see and commemorate.

The need to share my own excitement with an appreciative audience came to fruition after a visit to Partisan headquarters at their Tuscany headquarters in Florence, twelve years ago. We had been loading up on Chianti and schmoozing about the old days when Partisan Ennio Sardelli pressed me to write about his brigade's stormy past. Somewhat blotto from the heady Italian vino and feeling no pain, I hadn't comprehended that our convivial get-together would soon lead to a bonanza of reading material that ultimately overwhelmed my mailbox in California; yellowing records and journals that had hibernated in their dusty Partisan files for half a century.

Intermixing those historic documents with sparkling anecdotes I had gleaned from my unforgettable crony, Partisan Alberto Secchi, during the rich hours we shared off the line, it seemed that not proceeding would have been sinful.

More of their glorious history evolved as I began to write, aided with generous historic contributions donated by Italian war historian Claudio Biscarini and others who were insufficiently extolled in the acknowledgements that follow.

Map of Italy outlining its major provinces.

ACKNOWLEDGMENTS

This book would never have been realized without the assistance of American/Italian tutor Frank Fedeli, who assisted me by interpreting the many noteworthy documents received from Italian Partisan sources. He, along with World War II historian Claudio Biscarini, were my saviors when I needed to provide the reader with authoritatively correct information. Claudio is a collector and author of Italy's military history at the prestigious Cento Di Documentazione Internazionale Storia Militare in Tuscany. His informative tracts and photos kept arriving to complete the details needed to shed factual light on much of the data within these pages. They, along with the magnificent Partisan heroes who fought so gallantly in Italy, France and Yugoslavia, provided their gracious knowledge without expectation.

I will never forget Partisans Ennio Sardelli and Riccardo Barchielli, heroes who I had the pleasure of visiting at their headquarters in Florence. Their important contribution of archives were more than generous, and their encouragement led to the first of the promises I made to help in reactivating the waning image of their former glory days.

The warm friendship I shared with my Partisan buddy, Alberto Secchi, continues to flourish in my consciousness and haunts every page I've written.

I'm enormously indebted to David Honeck, a dear friend and retired English professor who mentored at Bentley College in Waltham, Massachusetts. He enjoyed reconstructing and correcting my crude phrasings, misplaced commas and other slips of the pen.

Famed author and screenwriter Harold Livingston enlightened me where to drop the adjectives and pal Jerry Epstein hovered apprehensively over my shoulder as I worked, offering inspirational nudges whenever I needed support.

Former comrade-in-arms and 91st Infantry Division historian Roy Livengood was most gracious with his exceptional memory and offered long-forgotten details of the grim war we shared.

And when my brains became too fuzzy to remember the elusive word or phrase I lacked, I knew that my astute confidante and inamorata, Bunny (Bernice Skolnick) would to speed me over those vexing writer's blocks.

Last, but certainly not least, I will never find words enough to express my feeling for Italy's remarkably sweet people. I was extremely fortunate to have experienced their surprising warmth and ingratiating qualities during our infantry's rocky road. Rare pleasures I had never expected in what could have been hell.

I thank all of you much more than this brief outline of appreciation could ever reveal!

CHAPTER ONE

In the Beginning

The Time: July 1944.

The Location: Italy's hilly terrain near the village of Chianni, sixty miles north of Rome. The rustic Tuscan expanse was a blend of surprisingly steep and thickly forested highlands separated by lush, orchard-filled valleys. All in all, a commodious defensive shelter for the concealed enemy.

The Situation: The American 34th Division had been there ahead of us and had completed their part of the mission. In need of rest, they were pulled off the line, leaving the battle-zone for our as-yet-untried 91st Infantry Division to finish the Chianni attack.

A ll hell broke loose on July 4, 1944 when the green troops of my battalion went on the offensive. The Germans, to our front, had known we were coming and had set their cunning traps for us with artillery zeroed in, machine gun nests and sinister minefields spread helter-skelter across our entire line of attack.

It soon became clear that the enemy owned the high ground and would be ready to slug it out with us on every peak and lush valley that had become Italy's killing fields. Ignoring the famed panorama that was Tuscany, our personnel vans and their drivers were long gone after ridding themselves of our foot-soldiers.

The first group of Partisans from the area of San Gimignano to join the fight against opression.

"Get the bastards!" they shouted above the roar of their motors as they left for a less dangerous area, their encouragement of no importance as we began the climb toward the crest.

The field around us was filled with battle debris and jagged-edged shell holes that bore witness to the previous hard-fought struggle, a sight that quickly aged us into fuller maturity as we passed the remains of fly covered, blood-soaked cadavers.

Aware of ever-present mines hidden just below the surface, we carefully followed in each other's footsteps. If the guy in front of you didn't "get it," the odds were a lot better that you'd both make it to the forward firing line positions and take your

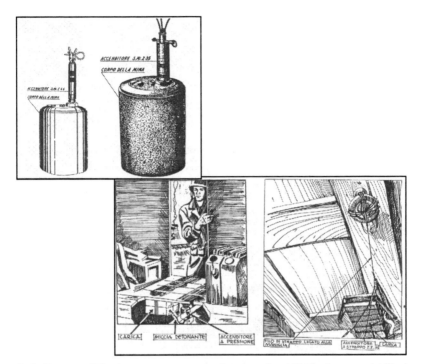

Left: German "S" mines were strategically placed to kill Partisans and Allied soldiers. *Right:* Two examples of German booby traps set for Partisans.

chances at "the front." In typical military fashion, company commanders had merely mentioned that our main push would be to capture the small village called Chianni, offering little detail about the battalion's first objective, Hill 634, that was also known as Mount Vaso. But that was the Army. Orders were orders and each of us had been trained to follow them without questioning.

First to advance were our scouting patrols. Those ballsy soldiers proceeded with masked fear about thirty yards to the front of riflemen, machine gunners and mortar men—infantrymen who were ready for the trouble that almost always occurred. Once the scouts made contact, generally by receiving enemy fire, each

platoon of soldiers that followed took up the fight in their prede-
termined positions. The sly Germans often waited for the scouts
to pass before opening fire, aiming for officers and lead elements
that had been caught off-guard before letting loose with everything in their arsenal.

The weather was stiflingly hot and clear during that Tuscan
July. Definitely an advantage for enemy observers at higher ele-
vations who waited to pick and choose their targets at will. At that
critical point, every man of us had been obliged to earn a master's
degree in the art of war the hard way, quickly learning to hate and
curse with an all-consuming passion.

It would take thirteen days to capture Chianni, but not without
the division suffering over a thousand killed or wounded.

Several weeks had passed before I would come to know of an
extraordinary force of heroes the title of this book extols; the
Italian Partisans. Their covert cells had recently begun to be known
and appreciated by inhabitants of Naples and Rome as they plagued
the German and Fascist tyrants with bold acts of sabotage and selective assassinations.

As valiant as our own infantrymen had been, the heroism of
the untrained Italian Partisans was becoming apparent and had
begun to be equally significant in their desperate battle to rid
themselves of the hated Germans. But their battlefields were different. Their unconventional procedure was to suddenly arise
from unsuspected locations beyond our lines where their veiled
presence wasn't likely to have been anticipated by the enemy.

At that time, I had yet to meet these special warriors on a
more personal level.

In their primitive beginnings, teams of Partisan freedom fighters
were trickling forth from residential neighborhoods in every part
of southern Italy. Anticipating an early linkup with approaching
Allied forces, small Partisan splinter groups of raiding parties

had been escalating their clandestine activities, all the while taking larger and larger nibbles out of the flanks of Hitler's army of occupation. But their intermittent bites lacked several important elements, among them a need for a greater variety of arms and organization.

At first, most Partisan efforts had been limited to distributing anti-fascist propaganda that meant little more than fleabites to Mussolini and Hitler's legions of occupation. But with the revitalizing Allied invasion of Sicily and new underground resistance groups confronting the Germans in Naples, new life had been infused into the Partisan upstarts. As the Allied invasion progressed, separate small Partisan resistance movements were beginning to form in the southern cities from among religious and political factions.

Those fraternal bands would ultimately coalesce to become one massive secular army of undaunted men and women. A stealthy freedom fighting force that, in the end, saved many American and British lives at a high, sacrificial cost of their own.

To this day, I still feel privileged to have participated in the last few acts of that wartime drama and to have befriended several of those magnificent Partisans who star in this narrative. Having enjoyed the fruits of their hard-won success, I've been amply rewarded to present this salient smattering of overlooked historic actions before their cherished memory passes into oblivion.

One young Partisan in particular had honored me on several occasions when I was given a five-day furlough to Florence. He had invited me to his home to break bread with his family during my battalion's winter stalemate and I took advantage of his offer, often visiting his home again on later leaves.

Alberto and I first met on an Apennine foothill prior to my regiment's attack against the mountainous German Gothic Line, and we quickly formed a mutual respect for each other that would turn into an unusually warm friendship. He, a roving Partisan fighter, and I, the 1st Battalion's Intelligence Sergeant. By then, I had gleaned enough of his language to converse with him, and he, like many other Italian students, had previously taken English courses in school. Along with others in his resistance group, Alberto had been sent to assist our infantry with the knowledge of the mountains we lacked, the steep and often treacherous zone that he and his comrades were more familiar with.

During the nine chaotic months I knew him, and as time allowed, we delighted in yakking about trivialities. We never spoke of it openly but I'm certain we both knew that both our lives rested on each other's abilities in the killing field.

While on a visit to Florence a half century later, I indulged my desire to visit the headquarters of any remaining Partisans, hoping to discover any records they might have had of my old friend. I wasn't sure if his group still existed and had lost touch with Alberto after VE day when we all went our separate ways, a customary disconnect among many war veterans anxious to return to our lives at home. Hopeful that there would be some kind of record keeping association in Florence, I left that task to my hotel concierge with enough of a tip to question the city's phone company's operator. Listening, I stood by, hanging on every word. Ten minutes later, we found that, yes, such an organization existed, but known then as A.N.P.I., unfamiliar initials that identified the Association of National Partisans of Italy. Fortunately, their office was only half-a-mile away, just beyond the southern bank of the Arno River.

I made haste for the address given, delighted that the once vital organization could still have existed. It was a pleasant twenty-minute walk from my hotel, but my spirits dampened when I found their office was located in a dingy, two-story stucco building. A tarnished brass sign near the entryway indicated what

I might find inside. My apprehension proved to be justified when I entered the dismal fifteen-by-twenty office and saw the remnants of their illustrious past.

But that pretentious mindset vanished with the thrill of introducing myself to the two pleasant occupants, Partisans Ennio Sardelli and Riccardo Barchielli, former Partisan brigade commanders who appeared to be manning the office.

I explained the purpose of my visit and their timeworn, wrinkled faces brightened up at the idea that this American visitor might be someone who could throw some sorely needed light on their former unsung glory. The two men jabbered among themselves, talking too fast for my knowledge of the language, something about the old times.

What they did make clear was that there weren't many of their group left, but that they were elated to see an American, someone who seemed to know and remember a lot about their past. With an inherent emotional wave of Riccardo's arms as he spoke, I was advised that their organization still functioned, but barely. They had been a gargantuan force for liberty in the bad old days, but what remained of their current membership had assumed a much less glorious role. Now it was limited to occasional meetings, record maintenance, with feeble attempts to rectify their former image of having once been a communist fraternity. At that exciting moment, I didn't really give a damn what their politics were. Noticing my reticence to discuss politics, the two made haste to reassure me that "In the beginning, most of us had been members, but soon there were many more that weren't so politically inclined." Obviously, their public relations record had suffered grievously in recent years, damaged to an extent that caused them much concern.

I don't recall that my friend Alberto had ever brought politics into our discussions or had any special axe to grind beyond despising Mussolini's Fascists and the Germans. I feel certain that, like mine, his single-minded creed had been limited to an ardent hatred for the despots we fought, eons beyond anything involved with theological or political dogma.

I studied the drab, office walls in the light of one sixty-watt bulb and one narrow, lofty window. Crimson and green velvet banners were draped around glass covered news clippings and hundreds of framed photos exhibited their revered dead.

The last shook me, rattling my composure as I studied them and battled the mountain-sized lump pervading my throat. Maybe I had turned soft over the years, but those revered soldiers had once been our brothers in arms. They, much more often than I, had probably taken on the worst of the war in the killing fields of Italy, battlegrounds that remain impossible to describe to anyone who hadn't been there, done that.

Ennio asked me to join them that evening, and on that note, we shook hands and warmly embraced in a typically emotional, Mediterranean goodbye. Of couse I'd be there!

Unfortunately, nothing could be found in their official records regarding Alberto.

Rarely noted in the narratives that follow, it must be remembered that simply by being an active Partisan, or even an evident sympathizer, the consequence of one's actions could place his or her family in harm's way.

Assumed to be guilty by association, the entire family would often be tortured, destined to suffer the same cruel fate as the culpable Partisan. As a result, innocent kinsmen retained a love-hate relationship with their heroes, and although highly appreciated, their nobleness was diminished with an ever-constant cloud of fearfulness. Although plagued with that double-edged sword that accompanied their heroism, the determined Partisans would find it a cold day in hell if ever they slowed their fight against the Germans, even if their families had to become casualties in the process.

Considering the formidable situation of the times, only a minis-cule amount of fragmented Partisan history follows in the pages allotted since volumes of their stories have remained lost or in-complete. After searching for and uncovering bits and pieces of timeworn anecdotes, there remained more than enough of their fascinating adventures to be explored here. First of the many loose-ended Partisan chronicles commenced after the Allies had invaded Sicily and were headed for the Italian mainland.

"Husky," the code name for the amphibious Allied invasion of Sicily, had concluded with the capitulation of the king's royal forces. Chaos and confusion followed as loyalist units of Italy's former militia were in the process of disbanding and many of those estranged soldiers and sailors headed for the port city of nearby Naples. Wherever they'd travel, they'd be enraged to see how Hitler's troops had overrun their country.

In groups of two or three, the demobilized Italian military re-turned to familiar territory and linked up with friends who had become members of the newly organized Partisan underground. Battle-trained soldiers augmented the tyro resistance groups with new and important knowledge in the use of weapons and martial arts, and not surprisingly, those bantam teams of insurgents be-came restless in their hunger to rebel against their German occu-piers. Even as they yearned for more action, their pent-up desire had to pause long enough to be fulfilled shortly afterward in 1943, when Allied Army soldiers neared the approaches to Ger-man occupied Naples.

Spent from having battled their way through hard-fought en-gagements against Hitler's militia in North Africa, Allied forces were ready to welcome any outside support, even when offered by the rag-tag, inexperienced Partisans. Any and all liberators were sure to be greeted as saviors in the war-torn city of Naples.

Although crippled by the lengthy German occupation, and devastating Allied air raids that had destroyed their invaluable seaport, Neapolitan residents had somehow restrained their mercurial temperament and anxiously waited for a chance to rebel.

For several months, an underground British Intelligence radio in Rome had maintained contact with the approaching Allied troops, and among other matters, kept them informed regarding the Partisan eagerness to contribute with acts of sabotage and mayhem.

Meanwhile, in an effort geared to maintain the upper-hand as Italy's clear-cut leader, ambitious dictator Mussolini had by then joined forces with the hated despotic German führer, Adolf Hitler. That amalgamation of ruthless tyrants had the effect of splitting the Italian populace into two opposing camps: Fascist, or anti-Fascist—with a minority of freedom-loving Partisan helmsmen covertly guiding the latter. Soon, there would be more—thousands more!

As a stand-alone fighting force, Mussolini's army of "Black Shirts" had become repugnant to the peace-loving Italians. The darkness of their tunics tended to convey their tactics and would become despised by a majority of their countrymen throughout the balance of the war.

With German cooperation and support, the Fascists segued into the image of a secondary army of occupation in Italy and quickly became known as enemies of the working class, jailing or killing any commoner they had a mind to. Their spies were everywhere, creating an aura of fear and distrust among the citizenry, let alone the threat of horrible torture and certain death when without trial, suspected Partisans were taken into custody. A virtual state of secrecy had become a cogent part of every Italian's life. Yet, a sizeable section of the population remained loyal to their Fascist dictator, and too often, would seize on any reason to apprehend the poor soul that uttered the slightest hint of anti-fascist sentiment.

Through the magic of secret radio, Partisan operators in Naples had begun to work in sync with the approaching Allies and were being strengthened with armaments and supplies parachuted to them by low-flying aircraft. Growing in confidence with each airdrop, freedom fighters were finding new vigor even as they witnessed the rape of their fair city.

German occupation forces had been planning to retreat with the arrival of fresh Allied troops, confiscating nearly everything of value in Naples and carting it back to Berlin. Something drastic had to be done, but waiting for the Allies to close in on the city wasn't enough for the Partisans. With patience nearly exhausted, bands of Partisans quickly organized a widespread uprising that was designed to catch the Germans off guard.

On September 26, 1943, an unarmed crowd of the populace streamed onto the streets of the city. To the bewildered Nazis, it appeared as if the entire city was participating. Masses of Neapolitans noisily protested in the streets wherever German garrisons were ensconced.

The following day, September 27, the Nazis retaliated with a heavy-handed roundup up of about 8,000 civilians, while in other areas of the city, hundreds of rioters took to the streets and began a series of armed counterattacks against the German troops. In the Vomero quarter of the city, one group of rebels initiated the onset of widespread revolt when they stopped a German Volkswagen and killed its driver. Fierce fighting followed in another section of the city as a former Italian Army lieutenant, Enzo Stimolo, led a charge of two hundred armed Partisan insurgents who raided a large weapons depot that was closeted in Castel Sant'Elmo, an ancient military fort at the high point near the harbor.

After the Germans called in reinforcements, the bloody battle continued, but Enzo's scrappy fighters weathered the enemy's return fire and ultimately captured the fort.

Later that first day of armed revolt, a wandering crew of Italian sailors prevented German engineers from carrying out their orders to place mines at the Ponte della Sanita. The enemy had hoped to cut off or slow down any Allied attempt to reach that important part of the city.

In the evening, a band of resistance fighters made an assault on another German supply dump and plundered the weapons store they would need for the historic days that followed.

On September 28, skirmishes around the city increased noticeably with the addition of more rioters who took part in selective massacres and street fights that had broken out around the docks and important public areas.

In the Materdei district, one group attacked a German patrol that had sought the safety of a large municipal building. The structure was soon surrounded by a horde of ungovernable rebels who kept it under siege for hours until the Germans sent in reinforcements and killed three of the rioters before they were forced to disperse.

Swelling Partisan squads continued to attack German garrisons and their patrols during which a group of forty armed freedom fighters set up a road block at Porta Capuana. Well-armed with rifles and machineguns, they killed six Nazi soldiers and captured four.

The Germans retaliated as they harassed innocent elderly men, women and teen-aged children, adding them to various German round-up sites that, by then, had resulted in an extensive accumulation of guiltless prisoners. The large mix of Neapolitan innocents and captured militants were assembled in a fenced-in, outdoor sports arena, but the German forces that still occupied Naples had been stretched to the limit with a minimal number of armed guards placed in and around the crowded soccer field.

Tempted to release the prisoners, heroic Lieutenant Stimolo reacted once more by surrounding the fence with an impressive assemblage of armed men when a white flagged truce was called. Oddly, he had been invited to meet with the chief of German operations in Naples, Colonel Hans Scholl, to negotiate the release of all Italian prisoners in exchange for an unfettered German retreat from Naples, free of all hostilities. The meeting, brought on by the unexpected strength of the Neapolitan rioters and their Partisan leaders, was readily agreed to and the prisoners were to be set free soon afterward. Until then, sporadic clashes continued to fill the streets on what was intended to be the last day of the riots.

With reports that the Partisan leader had participated in a pact that would allow the Germans to leave their city without unnecessary bloodshed, the desperate battle for Naples slowed to a standstill as the populace waited impatiently, hoping to see the long-awaited white-starred American tanks arrive.

Overnight, the German leader had brought in his own platoon of tanks, and in one of the city's most important piazzas, had attacked an assembly of fifty rebels, killing twelve and wounding seventeen. Obviously, any trust in the colonel's intentions no longer existed. A final show of German strength had been ordered.

During the early morning of September 30, the quiet neighborhood of Ponticelli awakened to thundering explosions generated by German artillery fusillades meant to be a warning for the workers to remain home and not participate in riotous actions. A warning intended to be observed from other parts of the city as well.

Those that dared leave the area were massacred by rifle or machinegun fire. As one of Scholl's last acts of defiance, his troops began their evacuation, almost as Allied forces entered the gates of the city. Fighting between the attacking army and retreating Nazi troops extended throughout the day as German artillery from the city's Capodimonte Heights continued to shell Naples.

Not far from the Port of Naples, along the coastal zone, other battles raged as the fleeing enemy left a trail of smoking ruins that included the burning of the city's important Historical Archives, which caused a grave loss of treasured documents.

At 9:30 a.m., October 1, the first Allied tanks entered the city, and by day's end, the commander of the German Army in Italy, Field Marshal Albert Kesselring, announced to the world that the German retreat from Naples had been successfully concluded.

As they left, the Germans let it be known that they had concealed long-delay time bombs in unsuspected, highly populated areas of the city. That alarming news had been corroborated by a captured German officer, who upon questioning admitted to having seen explosives wired into Naples' as yet unserviceable electrical system that had been put out of commission by previous Allied air raids. He also implied that they were set to detonate as soon as the power supply was turned on.

Word spread and the population of Naples was shaken once again. The first Allied infantry troops had begun their march into joyful Naples after the German withdrawal, but the enemy's reputation allowed for the fact that Hitler's army had been capable of committing needless butchery in the past. Anything was possible. With the probability of many civilian casualties, American general officers felt obligated to order a speedy evacuation of as many of the city's population as possible near the time the power would be returned. Their departure would include well over a million Neapolitans, including the sick and elderly.

Hospitals on the outskirts of Naples were already filled with infirmed civilians and newly arriving Allied wounded. Those who could manage to do so, walked toward the city's heights, while others were carried or driven as far away from the potential danger as possible. The tension grew as everyone waited for the power switches to be turned on. When it occurred, nothing out of the ordinary transpired.

Had the threat been a ruse? It wasn't too likely that there had been a miscalculation by German demolition experts since they were known to be masterful in the use of explosives. Yet, several had been set to detonate unexpectedly and did so weeks later when one fiendishly large antipersonnel bomb did explode, rocking the city's Central Post Office and causing seventy-two killed and wounded casualties.

It would take many days afterward for Naples to rest easier, hopefully free of the German villains at last.

Bold, unrecorded Partisan actions had taken place in and around Naples with an augmentation of sabotage the modern world had never known before. The badly battered metropolis had become the Partisan's first important training ground, but more action would follow. Much more!

Almost overnight, a significant number of heroic civilians— leaders to be in nameless battles yet to come—would take up new heroic roles throughout Italy.

News of their victory had spread through the country like wildfire, and would go down in the country's history books as "The Four Days of Naples." With that success, potential Partisan agents from every corner of the country revived their pent up vigor with anticipation. Aware of their newly gained repute, resistance groups converged into larger, more formidable brigades. Partisan leaders from Italy's south streamed northward into enemy occupied hills, dales and mountains as a cleverly concealed army of contention feared by their enemies.

With so much autonomous moxie ready to back them, the Allies and the newly-sprung American Office of Strategic Services (OSS) could now initiate deadlier stratagems their enemy hadn't counted on.

By the time Hitler's troops surrendered two years later, the disorganized Partisan cadres that evolved from Naples had grown into an impressive force of over 200,000 strong. What follows is an array of anecdotal reports, spiced with remembrances of their daring unconventional actions under fire.

A group of proud Partisans posing near Siena and the Casa Del Popolo, which they recaptured from the Germans.

CHAPTER TWO

Creation of a Hero

The Location: Across the foothills leading to Italy's Apennine Mountain Range and villages outside of Rome.

The Situation: Casualties had been mounting steadily for the Allied armies since the invasion of Sicily. Partisan involvement had become more noticeable with the added assistance of the newly arrived American OSS. My close friend, Alberto, would be among that group of Italian Partisans who put their lives on the line early in the battle.

Sleep was a rare luxury allowed the infantryman while his company was on the offensive. If not on patrol, guard duty or launching a night attack, he'd still find it extremely difficult to scrounge up the time and place to flake out.

Any hour of hibernation a man could seize after nightfall would seem heaven sent, but more often than not, the bone-tired soldier would be limited to a custom sized slit trench he had personally excavated out of the crusty, summer-dry soil.

As our battalion's Intelligence Sergeant, I assumed the right to abandon my forward observation post long after dark. Only then would I get my platoon back to headquarters. Observing at that late hour was an unconventional stint in which I hoped to catch the flash of a rare headlight in the distance that suggested a favorite artillery target—an enemy convoy. The few times this opportunity presented itself seemed well worth waiting for, but I could never know the full extent of damage I had hoped for.

Upon returning to our battalion headquarters a new set of chores began. The first was always the same, selecting a few men of my platoon to stand guard around the perimeter of our outpost. Those of us not on duty would guide food and ammunition mule trains to our scattered forward companies that were sprawled throughout our mountainous zone. With that out of the way, I'd see to it that Colonel Woods' maps and battle orders were ready for officers that would lead the coming attack.

Somewhere between those wee hours of the morning we were able to catch a few winks. It was there that I awoke about four o'clock one morning to find my Partisan friend, Alberto, kneeling in genuflection and crossing himself. As I attempted to envision the perilous mission he was about to undertake, he disappeared into the predawn blackness.

Hopefully, he'd return safely in a few days from wherever he and his group of freedom fighters had gone to harass the German Army. No doubt it was, as always, somewhere behind enemy lines.

Two weeks ago, he and several other Partisans had joined our infantry battalion as we readied an attack against the well-defended German Gothic Line. Already battle experienced and familiar with the area, Alberto's Partisan attachment had come to the aid of our infantry on several occasions in that unknown and easily misjudged territory.

Before joining us, our men had no knowledge that such a group of clandestine Italian combatants existed, but it wasn't long before I'd learn of their significance, and in the process, gain a companion I would never forget.

For whatever his reasons, Alberto lingered close to my side until the end of the war, disappearing at dusk or before dawn when he'd be off to some secretive sabotage mission. Operating on the edge of danger, he and his Partisans had survived with great difficulty as they tested and teased Hitler's extensive army of occupation; but too often, the enemy's reprisals took a weighty toll on those outnumbered freedom fighters. We could only wish these courageous men good luck and pray for success in their secretive assignments.

During the weeks and months we were together, Alberto would often reveal highlights of a sprinkling of Partisan raids that occasionally included names and locations of their hair-raising actions, allowing me to collect a smattering of those episodes chosen to be revived for this chronicle.

One of Alberto's earliest revelations occurred late one quiet evening after we had finished most of the *grappa* he had brought back from a previous mission. Somewhat inebriated, he offered me an inkling of his own initiation into the realm of Partisan activity that, oddly enough, began with his first bout of the shakes.

His initial acceptance into a cadre of freedom fighters included men of varying ages when twenty-one-year-old Alberto had dutifully followed instructions to meet them at 2:00 p.m. in a riverside bar near Rome's famous Castello de San Angelo.

Battle seasoned and wary, the five men had meandered into the saloon singly or in couples and sat drinking at the busy bar. Alberto had arrived early, warned by the leader not to attract undue attention. Fifteen minutes later, as Alberto searched for signs of the unfamiliar group, two of the men at the bar arose and moved to a table near the farthest corner, set down their drinks, shuffled and dealt a deck of cards that one of them had in his pocket. Another two who had arrived separately during those few minutes, sat at the main counter where the first two had left, and ordered beers. When their brews arrived, they too moved to the card game being played by the first two, stood behind the players and casually kibitzed.

Soon, the leader, who was the only one familiar to Alberto, also arrived. He, too, left his stool and casually sauntered across the room to where the men at the card game sat, stopping first at where Alberto sat alone, teasingly inviting him to test his luck at the game as well. As the next hand was dealt, four were at that table, with two, including Alberto and the leader, hovering nearby.

The Partisan leader bantered facetiously with the cardholders before whispering quick instructions for them to leave the bar slowly, just as they had come, and meet at his nearby flat in forty minutes. The leader's reason for the contrived meeting at the bar had been a precautionary move to ascertain that Fascist eyes and ears had not been drawn to Alberto and their upcoming mission.

Night found Alberto part of a team whose assignment was to derail a train. Partisan intelligence agents had reported that when it left the station in Rome, it would only be carrying a limited number of important German officers and Fascist chieftains to an urgent meeting in Bologna. The enemy's hurry-up trip had been ordered to discuss delaying actions designed to block Allied troops from advancing through several important mountain passes. Success of the high-priority German "Gothic Line" plan would permit sorely needed German troops and supplies in southern Italy to leave for the more urgently needed transfer to the Russian and Western fronts. The report also stated that the unannounced time of the train's departure would probably be between midnight and 1:30 a.m., which was not unusual since the Germans used every means possible to avoid being strafed by Allied aircraft that controlled the skies over Italy.

Faced with that tempting but urgent opportunity to quash the Nazi tour de force, the Partisan leader arranged for his men to arrive at a strategic location about thirty miles north of Vatican City.

After dark, most of the city's civilians preferred the safety of their homes since the road traffic would be minimal.

Motorcars and vans could often be stopped for inspection by German patrols at any hour of the night, but the shrewd leader knew of a local garage in Rome that harbored an outdated ambulance. In many ways it still resembled its former, more serviceable state. Intending to use it as a van, its present owner had previously painted out the large red-cross insignia it once displayed but never got around to removing the flashing lights or outdated medical paraphernalia within it.

Within an hour and still partially equipped, the old vehicle received a bogus red cross painted on its sides along with a borrowed gurney. It was now ready to carry the six men to their assignment—one to sit alongside the driver and three inside with a pretend patient laid out on the gurney—to their assignment. Hospital uniforms had been supplied to all but the patient. If stopped, an inspector would see the wet-looking bloodstain on the khaki blanket covering him as well as a massive, red stained bandage on the chest area of his partially exposed torso. No siren or disconnected warning lights would be used.

If intercepted at enemy road blocks, they'd appear to be medics and male nurses, and if necessary, make known that there was no need to use the siren and lights since the patient's neck and face would be made pale enough for him to appear at death's door. Alberto was chosen for that role, revealing later that he was sure the others had prayed as arduously he had done that the ruse would work. Every precarious gamble during those times had been a life or death risk to the desperate Partisans and sabotaging such an important target seemed well worth the very chancy effort.

Shivering in the back of the faux ambulance, Alberto couldn't help but feel panicky under his oversized hospital tunic. Even the warm night air wasn't enough to satisfy his nerves that were stressed to the limit.

Eleven p.m. Twenty-eight miles north of the Vatican, the group arrived at an advantageous site and covered the van completely with a camouflaged tarp. Well off the road in a clump of trees, yet near enough to make a quick getaway, it waited hidden until needed. After daubing their hands and faces with charcoal they took up positions along the track they intended to reposition.

Armed with heavy crowbars, four of the stronger young men took turns plying away at the rail near a point where it had been joined to a separating crossbar. The fifth man assisted the group leader who was more experienced in handling explosives, and completed the task by placing a large timed explosive charge alongside the track, seventy yards to the north of where the first four men worked to derail the train. Seconds after the train left the rails that blast would add deadly damage to the personnel cars behind the engine, crippling as many of their passengers as possible. After placing the explosive, the two men would act as lookouts for any roving witnesses that might interfere with the project in progress.

By a little after 1:00 a.m. their tension increased to a crescendo when they saw their leader lift his ear from the pulsating track to signal that their target was approaching. At its rate of travel it should arrive within eighty seconds.

After estimating the train's arrival time and double-checking a final touch to the bomb that would be primed to go off in pre-timed seconds, the six Partisans packed their gear and rushed to the hidden ambulance that would carry them to the nearby road and comparative safety.

Less than a minute had passed when the train's iron wheels hit the broken rail. Attempting to stabilize itself, the engine vainly teetered for a few seconds before leaving the tracks, soon to be followed by the smoky chaos that surrounded the personnel carriages when the delayed charge exploded. By the time of that terminating blast, Alberto and his Partisans were well on their way back to safety.

The sky above the tree line lit up for a moment like a quickly fading fireworks display, followed by the blast that was barely heard over the noise of the van's old motor from a mile away.

The Partisans had no time to observe the pandemonium that had gifted them the minutes needed to spread a comfortable distance between themselves and the smoldering coach cars. Alberto could only surmise the confusion that reigned towards the rear of the train as hostile squads of enemy soldiers rushed off to search the area. No one could have seen or reported seeing the fleeing ambulance as it took to unfrequented side roads towards the safety of an alerted Partisan hideaway five miles to the north.

The six men were effusively congratulated by the paint crew that had been waiting for them in nearby Narni, ready to spray out the van's temporary red crosses in the semi-darkness of their obscure garage.

Alberto's first mission could have been a completely satisfying success except for one exception; the elated Partisans couldn't have waited around long enough to enjoy seeing the damage they had caused their enemy. When he finished telling me of his adventure, he admitted to having been amazed by his leader's ability to pull off the sabotage so perfectly, and that he had been profoundly impressed with the importance of precise timing and organization. A valuable, life-preserving lesson that would put him in good stead later.

Compared to Alberto's frightful war, mine was almost always straightforward. If captured, American G.I.'s would usually be questioned before being taken to a prison camp till war's end.

But no gray area existed for the Partisan unlucky enough to be taken alive. He could always be assured of the worst kind of torture and death.

I was often curious about Alberto's previous life, and when the war finally ended on May 2, 1945, I couldn't resist asking, "What in the hell was it that convinced a nice kid like you join the Partisans?" His response shook me. As boozed up as we both were at that auspicious time, I received the revealing confession I hadn't been privy to before.

On that unreal afternoon of the enemy's surrender, we had been resting on the grounds of a former German prisoner-of-war site about twenty miles southwest of Venice. It would be hopeless to describe our emotions since words and overused adjectives for what every soldier felt on that day would be hard to find in any thesaurus.

Only yesterday we were ecstatic as we watched the strafing of British Spitfires and American P38s hammering away at the retreating Germans vainly attempting to get to the Alps. The echoing staccato rumbled on, offering a glimmer of hope that we wouldn't have to chase them from the Po Valley through those precipitous mountain passes. As far as the eye could see, immensely gratifying results of the steady strafing lay scattered all along the shoreline of the sluggish Po River. A maggoty stink pervaded the air and hung like an invisible fog that emanated from hordes of contorted blood-soaked bodies and fly-ridden mule carcasses. The nauseating stench was abetted by the rancid black smoke of smoldering Tiger tanks and halftracks, up-ended artillery pieces and splintered wooden drays with their dead, fly-ridden beasts of burden still attached.

Clearly the war was all but over and that overwhelming panorama should have justified triumphal shouts of joy, but only a repressed quiet could be heard as we moved past the satanic display. Perhaps it was our inability to suppress the memories of our own killed and wounded buddies that weighed heavily and prevented us from enjoying the precious moment. The unusual silence in our bivouac area was proof enough that every man of us felt the same.

Alberto, as well, seemed to be lost in the depths of a melancholic depression that appeared much deeper than our own. A startling contrast to what I would have expected since our own unfinished date for battle in the Pacific had yet to come, and his war didn't include Japan. One would have thought it to be the greatest day of my friend's young life, yet he certainly didn't appear to realize it.

Seeing him deep in some kind of funk was completely out of character for the man. The contagious smile was now a cold grimace, his mellifluous yakking now a sullen silence. Although I was aware that we both were a few sheets to the wind, I couldn't help but be shaken by my comrade's dejected appearance. Remembering him now, I'm reminded of how much this Italian paladin resembled American movie star Leonardo DiCaprio, even down to his charming grin and jaunty carriage. But then, he stared dewy-eyed at nothing as he squatted listlessly against the stucco building with white-knuckled fingers wrapped tightly around his bent knees. Obviously, the heartsick man was carrying too much of the world on his shoulders, but why?

"Why so sad, buddy? What the hell's goin' on?"

His soulful response shook me, especially when he stifled his voice to avoid breaking up. When he was able to answer, it was with a strange touch of anger in his voice.

"Bastard *Tedeschi* (an appellation used by Italians to specify Germans)! They stay too damn long in Roma, steal everything. Pretty soon nothing much left for our people. No rice. No meat. No real flour to make the pasta. We buy everything else from *brigata nera.* How you say, black market? Eggs, one dollar each! Rice, a hundred-seventy-five dollars a sack! Meat, chicken? Forget about it!

"Every day *bastardi* Nazis take people off street, even out of church. Send away to slave labor camp and never see again."

Alberto punctuated every reference to a German with a slight turn of his head as if to spit, and that he did often but dryly.

"*Sergente*, I have never speak to you about Edda...my sweetheart. I meet Edda in school. We study to be teacher when the whole crazy thing begins. Edda's papa was get killed fighting for *porco* Mussolini in Africa. Her mamma was *Ebraico*, you know, Jew...worried all the time if Gestapo find out. Her mamma make me feel bad because I am *Cattolico*, but Edda and me, we love each other very much and I know we find way to marry after war is finish."

He continued to complain about this dilemma while I waited for a convenient break in his story to offer him my canteen cup that still held a few ounces of tepid, boozed up coffee. He refused, showing dissatisfaction with my brownish concoction to let me know that his canteen held real *grappa*. After taking a deep slug out of his cup for himself, he poured me a healthy splash, relishing it even though it had the taste of aluminum. I couldn't have cared less no matter what it tasted like.

The brief pause over, Alberto continued to justify the reason for the depth of his doldrums. His inamorata had become ill during the winter cold snap and lost much of her weight, worsening her already depleted condition. It would have been practically impossible to bring her food since anything she could eat under her mother's dietary laws was highly limited, rationed or much too expensive. As for heat, coal was unavailable since the German officers had confiscated almost all of it for their own use.

Making matters more frustrating, Alberto could rarely find the means to bring her anything nourishing, leaving her mother to scavenge alone for subsistence. It seemed that almost every citizen of Rome was being deprived of food and warmth, but Edda's situation worsened with time.

Ridding Italy of the hated enemy occupation and rape of their country as quickly as possible seemed the only hope left, and by becoming a Partisan, Alberto assured himself that he would be doing the right thing for both, his ailing sweetheart and his country.

I had my answer.

And so another wonderful freedom fighter had been spawned, adding to the growing roster of Partisans who, for reasons of their own and love of country, would take a colossal toll on their enemy. This they accomplished in imaginative, uncharacteristic ways that their usual easy-going, romantic nature would never have previously considered.

It had been eight months before that historic VE Day when Alberto had first affixed himself to my battalion. At first, he seemed hesitant to fill me in on his mysterious activities, but soon, his ineffable trust in our affinity gave in, allowing me the cherished opportunity to learn more of his secretive exploits. Especially one of his first that I thought of as remarkable in its divergence from the usual.

Shortly after the incident of the train derailment, Alberto's subsequent boot camp assignments had been limited to traveling behind German lines to make contact with fledgling groups of resistance fighters that required assistance. After reaching and conferring with the newcomers, he'd communicate with his headquarters in Rome by radio, telling them where and what to send them in the way of arms and ammunition.

In the process of his job as a preparatory currier, Alberto's mentors assumed he would also learn of the group's early trials and tribulations in battle, which should materially affect his later, more challenging activities for the better.

During the first few months of Partisan existence there had been little in the way of organization among the small, roving bands of fragmented vigilantes. Some had gone to the extent of declaring elfin wars of their own as they attempted to harass the Germans, their bold attacks often ill-fated when they presumed to take on forces better prepared and much larger than their own.

Alberto assisted one such headstrong group near the country village of Civita Castellana, north of Rome. There, he'd assess their odd assortment of weapons that would never be enough to accomplish the task they had in mind. A coded call to Rome was all that was required to convince Alberto's quartermaster to send the novice group side-arms, machine guns and hand grenades. They would mysteriously arrive within a day or two, greased and ready for service, after which, he'd teach the excited men how to operate them.

Not that he had become masterful in their operation, but certainly, he was more knowledgeable in their use than the four Partisans who depended on him for what he, himself, had learned only a few weeks earlier in Rome.

Grimy old rifles and double-edged switchblades had been the first weapons of choice for the rural group since almost every Partisan already possessed those useful instruments, using them for such commonplace chores as butchering cattle and shooting prey. The four men he instructed were quick learners and could soon pass any test in the use of the newer American M-1 rifles and pillaged German hand grenades supplied by his headquarters.

Instructions from his superiors to Alberto had been explicit: "Allow the group to pull off their intended attack without your interference. Their plan of sabotage should be left entirely up to squad leaders who reluctantly accepted outsiders, and by all means, avoid the temptation to participate! Do your best not to mess around with their impulsive egos."

Although he was often tempted to do otherwise, he had his orders, and those he carried out with unfeigned respect for the graying, pot-bellied men of Dante's—the name of the small group's leader—zealous Partisans who seemed to accept the young outsider on their own terms.

For whatever reason, Alberto had been impressed with the men from their very first meeting. He explained to me that it was the first experience in his dealings with solo liaison errands.

The following story was divulged to me with all the inborn expressions of my friend's irrepressible passion, and transcribed here as if he had written it.

Dante's clique of potential warriors consisted of the four provincial peasants who had convened in a dirt-filled cave on the outskirts of the small town. At first glance, Alberto couldn't help worrying about their age and ability to pull off the plan they had been discussing.

Two of the four impassioned, raspy voices were belaboring a point, feeling safe that their cavern faced away from the road traffic and out of hearing range of German convoys or curious Fascist police. More than usual, enemy traffic had been using the town's rural byway on their retreat from Naples and Rome towards more northern positions in Tuscany and the coast.

Dante had become their unofficial leader and was clearly distressed as he berated Spada, one of the four, for wanting to deviate from his original plan.

"I don't want to argue," Dante said. "We hit the damn convoy first, then we'll have a better shot at eliminating the bastards at Pendini's."

"I see your point, my friend, but why in the hell can't we do both?" Spada shot back, his undulating arms joining in the disagreement. A remnant of what had once been a cigarette dangled from his lips as he continued. "It would be my greatest pleasure to personally handle Pendini's, and we know there are always at least seven or eight Fascist pigs and German officers filling their beer-bellies. You'd think the bastards never get tired of drinking beer. We'll still have more than enough time to handle the other business when I return, No? Let me do it tomorrow evening. Louisa will help."

With that eminent postscript that included his daughter's name, Spada's anxious eyes squinted hopefully at the two other men in the group, studying them for tacit signs of agreement.

Nothing would have pleased Dante more than killing off as many of the Huns and Fascists as possible, but at that moment he preferred to avoid Spada's wrangling. After all, the man did have good cause. But if anything adverse might happen to his larger plan, he'd resent it terribly.

All the men in the group had reason to annihilate their enemies, and when the shouting was over, they realized it would come down to a vote in the disputed issue. If Spada won, the leader would have to give in.

The group's body language hadn't changed. Spada had been Dante's best friend as well as the main explosives technician in the group. He would miss the man terribly if anything happened to him.

"You mean you would really be willing to sacrifice your sister?" Dante said, knowing the answer in advance.

"I'd offer up my sainted mother if it came to that, but I know my plan for Pendini's is almost foolproof!"

Spada could have eaten his words and knew full well he lied. He loved his aging mother too much to sacrifice her for the few lousy dead Germans he planned to kill.

"Louisa is smart," Spada insisted. "She knows how to follow orders. Let's vote on it already!"

Spada ended his last request knowing that it allowed the leader little choice. He had already guessed that his point would take precedence over Dante's since the hate for the Germans and Fascists had often been steeped in stark family tragedy, transcending everything else they held dear.

Alberto could only remain watchfully silent in the background as he waited.

It was no surprise when the two poker-faced men raised their hands in favor of Spada's supplemental plan. Ivaldi's vote had been assured since he had lost his youngest son to a bout with typhus during Mussolini's aborted Ethiopian campaign, and his eldest was imprisoned somewhere in Italy's north. That twenty-six-year-old youth had been arrested five months earlier by the Blackshirts for a facetious quip he had made about Il Duce's mistress. The Fascist's got wind of it and the boy hadn't been heard from since.

To a man they despised the very ground their dictator walked on, considering him and his bootlicking army as being worse than excrement.

Dante looked around and could only concede to his friend. "Well, I suppose you know what you're doing but we'll have to make provisions, in case...." The doleful words that followed stuck in his throat as he continued. "Carlo will pair up with me. Ivaldi with you. But make no mistake—all of us better be there to handle the fucking convoy according to plan. It might be our last chance to hit the scum before they cut and run, and I, for one, would certainly hate to miss this chance!"

With that, Dante glared at Spada and issued final instructions.

"After you finish at Pendini's, get your ass home. Stay there until you have to meet us, but with enough time to get to the pre-arranged location. We can't wait for you, so don't screw up or Ivaldi will have to work alone. Good luck tomorrow, *amico*. You know I only wish you the best, but remember, this may be our last chance to get them where it counts."

Unshed tears came to Dante's eyes as he held onto Spada's hand for an extra minute before they all dispersed to their home-steads. He might never see the man again if his projected sabotage failed.

Once again, he turned to Spada as the others left the cave, this time embracing him and blubbering, "You know we can't wait for you, dear friend, so for God's sake, don't fuck up! I'll pray to the saints that everything works as planned."

Alberto had become close to these aging men and smiled in-wardly, joining them in that last touch of sentiment.

Dante's final instructions were redundant since everyone had already memorized the operation. They all knew the odds against Spada's safe return and would pray often and fervently for his success during the next comfortless hours. Through the weeks of planning and arguing, those self-made heroic Partisans had probably never given much thought to their own mortality, at least, not in the open. Questioning their apparent lack of fear, I was assured by Alberto that their deceptive swagger was in its smallest part, real.

Rain had been forecast and the following afternoon the sky turned dark and cloudy. At the last minute, Spada changed his plan. He needn't use his sister for a decoy since his new course of action would be simpler. She wasn't required now so why risk her life unnecessarily. All he needed from her before she left would be to drive him into the village where he would make his way to Pendini's...alone.

Spada picked up the old accordion that had become heavier with explosives and threw the weathered leather strap over his shoulder, shuddering noticeably when the bomb-laden instrument made contact with his body. It would never again be playing the tarantella he once loved.

His sister had dropped him off near Pendini's bar at 6:00 p.m., and as instructed, quickly left the vicinity. Before entering, Spada slipped into the entrance of a nearby alley and set the timing fuse for eight minutes, knowing full well he'd have to act fast or martyr himself to the explosion. He looked around to be sure there were no window shoppers nearby and noticing nothing to dissuade him, parted the beaded drapes at the entrance and took a seat at an empty table inside with the innocent looking, musical squeeze box on the floor at his feet.

Looking around, he was forced to squelch a grin. Due to the weather, the attendance inside appeared larger than usual. Most probably, the rain had prevented customers from sitting in the outside patio which could have created a major problem when he'd attempt to leave

One of the tables held three of the village's prominent Fascists, and at least half the other tables had small groups of German officers indulging themselves in Pendini's popular *risotto con funghi* and beer. The more the merrier, he reasoned. It only made the risky business more worthwhile.

No one in the restaurant seemed to have paid him more than a passing glance. In five minutes he'd be gone, leaving them all to their respective hells. But his momentary musing was shattered when he was unexpectedly startled by one of the German officer's near him.

"Hey, *paesa*! Play us something on your music box."

Shaken, Spada had to think quickly. Get the hell out now or gamble that the German might be a bit more patient.

"Certainly, *Herr Capitano*, but I always eat first. Then I can perform at my best when I'm not hungry."

"*Ja, ja*! Eat, by all means. Waiter, bring this man something to eat. He looks thin, skinny as an organ grinder's monkey."

The men at the officer's table laughed since Spada's full-bodied configuration could never be mistaken for lacking in food.

Spada knew the bar well, having visited it often in better days. The clock on the wall showed 6:15 p.m. Three and a half minutes had passed and he couldn't wait much longer. When five minutes and twenty seconds had elapsed, Spada made his move.

Taking advantage of the German's agreement that he could eat first, he grasped at the chance to make his getaway. Quickly ordering another drink, he loudly asked the waiter where the toilet was, knowing all along that it was in the shadowy, unlit hallway at the back end of the bar. Leaving his accordion at the table, he casually left the table, opened and closed the latrine's squeaky old door, then quietly exited through the back door.

Without wasting another precious second, he entered the commercial alley behind the building and made tracks for the narrow corridors he had previously familiarized himself with. He ran through the rain as fast as his feet would carry him on the wet pavement, and although chubbier than the norm, the daily fieldwork at his farm had kept his muscular frame in satisfactory condition. With the extra adrenaline needed to get away from the violent scene, he had already covered a hundred yards in near-record time before shortness of breath forced him to slow down. But that was long enough for him to hear the blast. The momentary flash blended with lightning strikes that created their own brilliance as they reflected off the clouds.

Later that evening, when he arrived at Dante's prearranged location, he barely had time to tell the group about the breathtaking few moments when the cloud-darkened sky above the village had lit up. After congratulating him, the men agreed that they, too, thought they heard the explosion as it sent an unexpected gust of fire-warmed air against the village's perimeter.

Dante had to admit that it was like music to his ears, and that the old accordion had blasted out its best and last note into one deafening crescendo. "A beauty!" he shouted. "The loudest music

I ever heard! I'll. buy you a new accordion when we're finished here."

Spada grinned, and full of self-approbation, said, "A few gawking spectators were out in the rain so I stopped for a few seconds and made believe that I, too, was interested in the smoke coming from Pendini's."

He related how he had picked up his pace after leaving the scene, urged on by Dante's words, "Get your ass back in time," a cogent order that repeated itself with each quickened step as he ran. He didn't need the hypnotic reminder knowing he'd have the whole group to face if he didn't make it back to their rendezvous by 9:30 p.m.

Alberto had been moved by Spada's story, particularly the heavy-hearted part that followed. I had become aware of how sensitive Alberto and the rest of his lion-hearted Partisans could be when, glassy-eyed, he told me of the touching episode that followed.

Spada let it be known to the waiting group that when he returned home to change clothes from his experience at Pendini's, the high pitched wail of sirens rushing by had left him with a feeling of exultant jubilation he hadn't felt in years.

His wife, Ernestina, had already guessed of the dangers he faced and crossed herself twice as he readied to leave for the next mission. He blushed as he divulged that he kissed her more passionately than usual when he left, and vowed dewy-eyed that he'd spend whatever time his saint's might allow him to pay more attention to her in the future, show her the affection she probably had missed. He was immensely elated with his coup but wouldn't have time to celebrate the victory before the next raid—if all went well.

Reports in the village later stated that a dozen people had been killed in the explosion, or so badly wounded they'd never recover.

There were now eight German officers and four Italian collaborators that were well on their way to meet their maker, hated
devils the Partisans would never have to concern themselves
with again.

Two years earlier, Spada had been a placid individual until he
received news that Mussolini's Fascists had arrested his only
son for leaving his military post in Messina. The young soldier
had attempted to visit the hospital from where his pregnant wife
had called to tell him that she might miscarriage. Ultimately, the
child was born but Spada's son had been sent to an unknown
slave camp in the north. Uppermost in Spada's mind was the
hope that his grandson would get a chance to know his father
once the country had been cleansed of its tyrants. Relating it to
himself, Alberto was quick to understand Spada's do or die savagery and understood.

As they readied to take their field positions, Dante's remaining
three men had only a few moments left to pat Spada on the back,
affectionately acknowledging the achievement of their comrade
before carrying out their next act of defiance, a dicey hit-and-
run attack against the next convoy of German troops that would
be expected to retreat northward that night.

Having made note of Spada's success at Pendini's, Alberto
reported it back to his headquarters in Rome. There, the sabotage
would be entered into Partisan records as a fortuitous gift, and
the return message simply wished the group the very best of
luck for their coming operations.

All four Partisans realized that this next, highly dangerous
mission had trouble written all over it from the beginning. A life
and death gamble. Well aware of the stakes if everything didn't
work out as planned, Dante's desperate Partisans had gone to
extremes to arrange their chances, but hardly anything in war is
ever perfect and Spada's recent accomplishment would be tragi-

cally tempered when several bullets ripped into his body that fateful night.

Alberto's narrative described what occurred at the time of the attack. He had received word from headquarters when the motorized convoy left its depot in Rome. By departing after 10:00 p.m. the Germans would avoid daylight and its concomitant Allied air attacks. Size and armaments of the convoy were not made clear, but for reasons of their own, each of the brave four had volunteered for the hit, run and hide mission. Each knowing full well that they were risking their lives if the convoy included a larger procession than expected, in which case their small group could easily be overwhelmed. They could only hope that it would be like most of the other eight vehicle contingents that had been retreating through the village's two-lane road.

Later that night, the men met at their pre-designated locations. All four carried automatic rifles and hand grenades rushed to them from Alberto's Partisan base. He had taught them how to use the unfamiliar armaments, and after a short session of instructions, wished them success as they left.

Dante had decided that it would be best to hit the enemy from two different points, one pair of men at the front, the other group, two hundred yards up the road, hopefully near the caravan's tail end. At a signal, they would jump the convoy in unison. Although outnumbered, they would do as much damage as they could within the allotted time before hightailing out of sight. Having been apprised by the radio that the night would be moonless and overcast, they hoped to quickly escape through the familiar approaches of tree stands and dense fields of tall, ripened cornstalks that led away from the country road.

As they waited for the arrival of the convoy, Spada and Ivaldi kept themselves busy readying homemade Molotov Cocktails. Those fiery grenades had recently been designed by the Russian

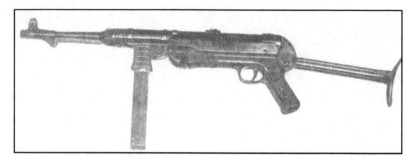

The infamous "Burp Gun." The German MP Maschinenpistol, also known as the "Zipper Pistol."

Army to destroy German tanks and had also been known to serve extremely well in raids on personnel carriers and open-roofed cabriolets that were known to transport ranking officers.

The men were grateful for the wet, pitch-dark night that worked in their favor. With Spada's return, every part of their plan was ready but no one counted on the enemy's surprising countermove that had come into effect.

In recent days, they found that too many of their troop movements had been detained by Partisan ambushes and the Germans had just begun to counter those actions with scout-led motorcyclists to lead their caravans. All motorized processions were to use the two-wheeled bikes to reconnoiter and be aware of any off-road shenanigans that might occur.

As their expected convoy passed through Civita Castellana that night, two noisy motorcycles crisscrossed the muddy fields, one on each side of the road. As expected, the contingent wasn't a large one since many roads were being used for the Wehrmacht's retreat. Their convoy consisted of one noisy half-track, two mobile 88mm cannon carriers, two canvas-covered personnel

carriers filled with officers and five trucks loaded with infantrymen. No cabriolets.

Spada and Ivaldi waited nervously inside an unused, partially
roofless storage shed, twenty-five yards off the shoulder of the
road. The two were readying for the right time to hit the forward
end of the caravan in order to distract the attention of the convoy
away from Dante's second squad, which was positioned up the
road. Dante and Carlo waited there in a camouflaged, brush covered culvert, armed with grenades and Molotovs, ready for the
confusion that would follow after the attack.

The roar of approaching motorcycles drew closer, and the first
two Partisans held their breath as they hugged the inside wall of
the dilapidated wooden shack, tommy guns at the ready.

The first enemy cyclist had stopped to urinate against the outside wall of the shack. On the opposite side of the road, the roar
of the other reconnaissance cyclist had combined with the convoy's traffic to deaden the sound of Ivaldi's footsteps as he
moved toward the urinating German. Being the nearest of the
two, he pulled his knife from its leather holster and attacked the
astonished corporal, aiming to slash his throat. The corporal was
almost a foot taller, younger and considerably brawnier than the
older Italian, and reached for the automatic rifle dangling from
his shoulder. The German managed to block Ivaldi's slashing
thrust but his automatic response groped for the trigger. Those
few mini-seconds were just long enough for him to press off a
few wild shots before losing his life to Ivaldi's second slash.
The element of Partisan surprise had been short-circuited and it
was now every man for himself.

The other cyclist heard the shots, and with his rapid fire
Schmeisser drawn and ready, made for Ivaldi's shack. In the
blinding glare of his floodlight he barely made out Ivaldi and
Spada as they rushed in opposite directions to make their getaway

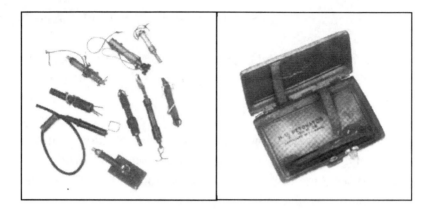

A variety of detonation devices used by the Partisans in the booby traps they set to wreak havoc on German supply and troop convoys.

towards the nearby field of cornstalks. Racing his motor, he sped towards the slowest of the two, catching Spada's more conspicuous form in the beam of his headlight just long enough to aim and shoot him down. Faster and younger, Ivaldi was further away, and by now had made it well into the visual protection of the stalks before he could be hit with the rapid spray of bullets that followed his trail.

With the Partisan's plan in chaos, Dante and Carlo had little choice but to remain concealed until the convoy left.

The sound of rapid-fire weapons continued to bark their deadly tattoo into the cornfield as the remaining cyclist raced up and down the edge of the field, occasionally triggering wild bursts after his unseen prey.

Dante was a practical man and realized that his attack had to be aborted. It would have been suicidal to continue since the entire German convoy had become alert and active. He cursed and knew there would be no points for becoming a martyr and prayed as never before for the well-being of Spada and Ivaldi. It wouldn't make sense to wind up dead and his better judgment restrained him from continuing the attack. Other opportunities might come. There was nothing left he could do but remain shivering in the frigid metal culvert until the hateful bastards left.

With no hope to regroup, and the apparent haste of the German convoy to rush ahead to their assigned destination in Tuscany, Dante could only wait there with Carlo. When the last of the enemy's convoy was safely out of sight, they raced toward his barn where Alberto waited feverishly for news.

Courageous actions taken by other Lilliputian bands of Partisans would always have their share of failures as well as successes, and no war had been entirely one-sided. Unfortunately, Dante's war had started with considerably less than fifty-fifty odds to overcome.

Wondering about the sounds of battle and not privy to what occurred, Alberto could only remain on the sidelines to wait for the results of the skirmish from a safe distance.

Spada's body was recovered before dawn, left bleeding in the brush by the time-pressed, retreating Nazis. He was buried in his family's pasture instead of the churchyard, and only Alberto, the other three men of his action group and Spada's small family attended the funeral. No one else in the village would be notified of the hero's secretive interment since the local Fascist police would be on the watch for whoever might have been Spada's extended kin and associates.

Two nights later, the three remaining men met at their cave. In memory of their fallen comrade they passed around a jug of potent *grappa* and drank to some vague future attempt, vowing to try again but better prepared.

Soon, and with only a few more such hazardous ventures under his belt, Alberto requested that his commander permit him to become involved with more precarious, soul-satisfying actions in which he could take a more active role. That time couldn't arrive soon enough to satisfy him.

Louisa, Spada's spunky forty-six-year-old sister took his place in the group a few weeks later and was never captured. To be caught alive would be equal to the worst kind of death at the hands of their sadistic captors. She promised her mourning sister-in-law that she would try to take special care during whatever actions she would become involved in, and according to Alberto, she did.

More than usual, he seemed interested in the family's progress and gleaned that Louisa had learned to make explosives, ultimately becoming expert in their distribution by spreading the technical information along to other groups.

With unrelenting hate in her heart for the Germans, Louisa had become known to create an art form out of constructing deviously powerful killing devices by making them look as if they were something other than what they were. To the enemy's utter frustration they could appear anywhere: a harmless box of sweets left on a counter, a timed wad of sticky goo slapped onto a shipping crate or concealed surreptitiously under the chassis of a vehicle. There would be nothing too outlandish in the way she chose to kill, since neither side had been interested in taking prisoners.

Following the woman's Partisan progress regularly, Alberto described her gallant, selfless activities to me on more than one occasion. Most often she'd vent her hate on the enemy's transportation systems, such as trucks, trains and martial vehicles that strayed too near her village. Obviously, she and others like her had probably shortened our battalion's stay in Italy by no small degree.

Soon after Dante's aborted attack, all German troops had left the south and retreated into the protective hills and valleys of verdant Tuscany. Partisan exploits in Rome had tapered off with younger, more vigorous freedom fighters migrating to cells in Italy's north. Dante's gallant group from Civita Castellana resumed their gentler life in the village.

Louisa's special talents were requested by a newly formed brigade that had begun operations near Viterbo, forty miles north of Rome. With few ties holding her, she left her village to continue avenging her brother's death elsewhere.

Spada's jailed son had not been heard from. Hopefully, he would have been repatriated after the war to help his family run the farm and fulfill his father's wish for him to spend time with and enjoy his three-year-old youngster.

With his solo mission in Civita Castellana concluded, Alberto would continue similar assignments before it became necessary to rejoin his group in Rome in time to greet the approaching Allies.

Grim warning from the German command, posted in Perugia, listing the names of
Partisans captured and condemned to death.

CHAPTER THREE

Life and Death in Rome

The Time: Early fall 1943 to summer 1944.

The Situation: Thirty-six thousand Allied soldiers had breached the Gulf of Salerno. Called "Operation Overlord," the landings occurred a short distance south of Naples where Allied forces had broken out of the Salerno beachhead with heavy casualties. Italy was in utter turmoil and the economy was in ruins. Optimistic Partisan commanders expected imminent airborne landings in Rome, Tuscany and Milan. German soldiers surrounded the Vatican. Mussolini's demoralized army had lost 300,000 men in Africa and Greece. The dictator planned to move his headquarters from Rome to the safety of Lake Garda in the north, and only Italy's Fascist "right" remained loyal to him. With the Resistance Movement having retaken Naples, other belligerent Italians had begun to organize Partisan groups in Rome.

Documents and hastily scribed records would occasionally provide terse Partisan notes. Too often, however, there was nothing at all regarding their actions. It was understandable that information written on the run would leave us wanting, but those actions that had been recorded made for a fabulous history. Unlike the names of worthy individuals that were unrecorded during Naples' Partisan uprising, a sparse but satisfying number of graphic documents had been retained in Rome. Some short, others random, but all of great interest. The paucity of Partisan communications from German controlled Rome began at a time between the landings in Sicily on July 9, 1943, and mid-October 1944, when war operations in Italy had to be drastically slowed to accommodate needs for the D-Day invasion of Western Europe. During this period, it was difficult to send American OSS missions into enemy territory. Liaison with the scattered, clandestine forces had been too hard-pressed to accomplish since efficient German forces exercised rigid control over that area. At that time, the OSS was still in its infancy and there were few radio operators and meager means for controlling their undercover missions.

Everywhere, new Partisan formations were increasing daily, so rapidly as to create huge organizational difficulties, and as yet, not enough arms and ammunition had been sent.

During the fall of 1944, the situation changed for the better. Not all plans could be successfully carried out. One of Rome's last living Partisan commanders, Roberto Guzzo, stated in his records that his brigade had lost four hundred two men and women through execution, killed in action or deported to German slave labor camps, never to be seen again. But we must gather that a considerable amount of retributive damage would have been inflicted upon Guzzo's enemies that were not listed in these and other reports we received.

Another Partisan, Rosario Bentivegna, reported that from September 8, 1943 to June 4, 1944, the Roman resistance movement had hidden or protected 400,000 European citizens. His records state that among those, 4,000 persecuted Romans had passed through German and Fascist jails with 1,000 of those resulting in deaths. Another 2,100 of its Jewish citizens never returned from camps of extermination.

"Tommaso Moro" was the lyrical pseudonym assumed by another small, but efficient group of Partisan heroes that had disguised themselves as soldiers of the P.A.I., a loyal branch of "Police Africa Italian." Because sporadic shreds of Italy's demoralized regular Royal Italian Army still existed, a dozen Partisans had pilfered the necessary number of police uniforms and freed their captured comrades who were condemned to death by a German military tribunal. Unlike others to come, we were unable to discover the records of just how that remarkable feat was accomplished.

Numerous successful Partisan raids continued until on December 6, 1943, when Antonio Poce led a massive distribution of "Bandiera Rossa"* anti-Nazi pamphlets into 120 of Rome's most popular cinemas. In it, he described the indiscriminate plundering of art and decorative furnishings that had been filched by the Germans. Several Partisans in his group had been caught and arrested while attempting to stop the thievery. One, Ezio Malatesta, a twenty-four-year-old journalist, was summarily imprisoned. The harrowing story of his trial and execution is recalled from Partisan records.

His one-sided trial started the 28th of January. The foregone sentence was issued on the 30th and carried out on the 2nd of February as Enzio stood tall in front of a host of officious looking, uniformed functionaries. The young journalist admitted to everything he had done, declaring he was proud of his actions, and when deliberately provoked by the public accuser, he spat in his face to demonstrate his defiance.

---

*During the summer of 1943, one of the largest Roman Resistance movements had assumed the colorful Partisan title of "Bandiera Rossa" (Red Flag), an appellation derived from a clandestine, anti-fascist tabloid that had been widely circulated by Roman Communists. That left wing group would ultimately number in the thousands and operate aggressively throughout Italy until the day Hitler's army surrendered.

Partisan documents continue, relating how the Fascists wanted to make an example of him, along with several others on trial. Unfortunately, his fate was in the hands of German judges. Predictably, they wasted no time in issuing an instantaneous death sentence to be carried out by a firing squad. The condemned prisoners passed their last days together in a single cell, and one, Jacopini, wrote this pathetic note to his mother:

> Dear, adored Mother,
> I never believed I could give you so much pain, but destiny wanted it to be this way, so I ask forgiveness from you and also my dear brothers, sisters and friends.

At dawn, eleven prisoners were brought to Forte Bravetta to face an Italian execution platoon. Among them was Partisan Colonel Luigi Rossi, who was to be shot by the Fascist soldiers. He viewed the executioners with disgust and shouted, "It pains me that it will be you Italians and not the Germans to shoot me. May God forgive you!"

Another hero of the condemned group, Ettore Arena , told them to remove the blindfold from his eyes and shouted, "I want to see those that kill me! Shoot me in the chest, not at my back. I am not the traitor. You are!"

So much strength of spirit impressed the execution platoon that many of their shots were directed at the ground or at the legs of the condemned. A German medical officer intervened with his pistol to give those who were only wounded a final *coup de grace*.

A myriad of other martyrs followed during the German occupation of Rome, including one of the luckier surviving Partisans, Corvisieri, who reported that on the 3rd of February, twenty-four hours after the execution of Malatesta and his companions, the German command covered the city with manifestos that in-

Partisan heroes Vasco Perugini, Rino Chesi and Enrico Rampinelli remembered in a graveyard near Siena where they died.

formed the Romans what had happened and warned them to re-
nounce any form of resistance. "Better to transform yourselves
into informers," it stated. Ignoring the warning, Bandiera Rossa
Partisans continued to take out their revenge in multifarious
ways.

****

Lido Duranti's life had never been easy. At the age of twenty-
one he, along with his older brothers, had been drafted into the
Italian Army to serve Mussolini's aggressions in North Africa.
During the final disintegration of the dictator's overseas army,
Lido returned to his family's countryside home in a suburb of
Rome, the bottom of his feet badly burned by the hot sands of
the Sahara desert. It took months of constant attention by his
mother for him to heal well enough to find a job at the Pirelli tire
factory where the Germans were in control of various products
destined to be used for their military vehicles. Almost immediately after being hired, Lido enlisted in a Partisan brigade, but
due to the diligence of German and Fascist patrols in command
of the plant, his Resistance group could do little to sabotage their
equipment. Frustrated, and anxious to hit the enemy where it
would hurt, Lido quickly organized his own group of men, friends
he could trust. From that time forward his troupe carried out numerous clandestine activities, one of which was to harass the
Germans that were retreating northward towards the art-filled
Tuscan city of Florence. With large, existing garrisons of Fascist
and German military personnel already stationed in the Roman
capital, it was urgent that their caravans should move through
the city rapidly. Any human error along the way could become a
titanic traffic problem if not handled with their usual efficiency.
After careful planning, Lido's dedicated Partisans were ready
and waiting at core positions, but as always, aware of sharp-
eyed German patrols.

Partisans dressed as Fascist police directed artificially created traffic jams that choked the main roads out of Rome. German vehicles were obliged to detour through residential, single-lane side streets, forcing their personnel conveyers to follow. Finding themselves isolated, smaller processions of ambushed enemy vehicles would run into prearranged nests of armed Partisans plying hand grenades and machineguns.

Residents of Rome would never forget how much those heroes had done for the town's esteem as they beheld the transformation of their activist citizenry into the heroic armies of killers. All this prominence could not have come without the cooperation of less noticeable civilians who were rarely in the spotlight, such as telephone operators, cooperative police and *medicos*.

Regarding the latter, copious praise is offered posthumously to one such hero, thirty-seven-year-old Maria Teresa Gullace. Maria, along with a number of other selfless, working women, had been a vocal demonstrator for the release of Partisan prisoners previously imprisoned for trifling transgressions, such as delivering tracts or carrying signs that criticized their enemies. At that time, the Fascists were in need of a scapegoat, and among others, Maria was selected to be executed by a Fascist marshal in front of the barracks of Mussolini's 81st Fascist Infantry on Rome's Via Giulio Cesare. With her death, the Italian women in the city arose in silent protest to aid the Partisan cause by establishing their own brigades. Several chapters in this book will process those developments, demonstrating their significance as premiere heroines in Italy's battle for liberty and justice.

****

During the many months of Rome's German occupation, Fascist puppets considered it fair game to exploit their power by victimizing any hapless citizen they took a dislike to. With tempers running high, it had become much too easy to be imprisoned,

Partisan hero Lido Duranti. *Right:* The memorial presented to his family after his death in 1944.

tortured and killed, or sent to unknown destinations for use as slave laborers. The infuriated population finally reacted on March 23rd, 1944, when Mussolini's Fascist squads were preparing to celebrate the anniversary of their initial march on Rome in 1922. Many high officials participated, protected by the 11th Company of a German *polizei* regiment that was commanded by an infamous Nazi leader, Major Dobek. His men were not the hated SS, but ordinary police who shared their parade with 156 Nazi soldiers and sang German songs that infuriated the Italian spectators along the viewing promenades.

No one but the Partisans had been aware that a young medical student, Rosario Bentivegna, had masqueraded in the uniform of a street cleaner, and in response to the parade, placed himself and a former garbage container in front of Palazzo Tittoni at two o'clock in the afternoon. Within his innocuous looking wheeled cart he had stashed eighteen kilos (forty pounds) of TNT.

Other Partisans were in on the ruse and were already in position

Ultima lettera ai genitori:

Siena 13 Marzo 1944

Cari genitori

Vi faccio sapere queste mie notizie le quali ho avuto la confessione perchè io sono condannato a morte spero in breve tempo di avere la grazia.

Ma sarà ben difficile state tranquilli non pensate a me se muoio la mia disgrazia è questa.

Ora vi saluto tutti in famiglia addio addio.

P. Simi

Addio cari genitori

addio addio

addio babbino e mammina

PRIMO SIMI

Classe 1925

Morto in seguito a sentenza di fucilazione eseguita nella caserma " La Marmora „ in Siena, il 13 Marzo 1944.

I genitori dolenti offrono questo ricordo del loro unico figlio Primo che con l'animo già compreso del puro ideale della redenzione nazionale, da iniqua sentenza di arbitrario tribunale ebbe recisa la vita nell'età più bella.

Partisan Primo Simi was captured near Siena and condemned to death. In this letter to his family, he told them he had confessed to his crimes in the hopes that his sentence would be reduced. It wasn't. Just before his execution, he asked his parents to forgive him for the disgrace he brought to his family by confessing.

to create chaos for the marchers at a preselected time. Francesco Curelli was between the Tritone and the Traforo, Pasquale Balsamo under the Messaggero building, Silvio Serra was near the Propaganda Fide. The Partisan list also included Franco Calamandrei, Carlo Salinari and Carla Bentivegna.

Soon the parade approached the busy center. When the time was right, Rosario casually lit his pipe, opened the cover of the garbage can and touched off the waiting fuse. Then, with barely enough time to spare, he left the cart and gingerly walked toward Quattro Fontane. A huge explosion rocked the center of the city, and from where they were positioned along the wide boulevard,

Partisans hurled hand grenades at the dumbfounded parading German regiment.

Everything stopped.

Not knowing what to do, everyone in the procession dashed headlong towards the nearest cross street, Via Rasella, a gradually narrowing avenue that would become a slaughterhouse for the disorganized Germans.

Notes in Partisan records state that "pieces of Wehrmacht uniforms and mangled cadavers were scattered all over the street. Later, the German casualty list showed thirty-two killed, with an additional fifty-four wounded."

Having assumed that the attack had come from above, soldiers that survived were ordered to open fire toward the upper apartment flats that lined the street.

German Commander Maizer had been drinking, and in his usual state of inebriation, wanted to destroy the entire neighborhood and kill everyone in of its inhabitants. A sober superior was able to convince him otherwise, but his staff of officers insisted on punishing the Romans that watched the riotous scene from their windows. An unknown number of innocent suspects were promptly collected and lined up with hands on their heads in front of the gate of Palazzo Barberini.

A call was made to Berlin where the usual barbaric response to "shoot them all" was received and quickly carried out.

****

In the spring of that year, a band of young Partisans had attacked a detachment of hated police, and with pent-up wrath, killed or wounded seventeen of them. It was immediately after that when a shocking new public mandate arrived from headquarters in Berlin: A terse warning that ten Italians were to be shot for every German killed. It would be the beginning of many infamous massacres to follow.

On March 24, 1943, an assembly of 335 Italian prisoners and protesters were summarily lined up and executed at Rome's Ardeatine Caves. Among them was the recently captured Partisan hero, Lido Duranti. It was assumed that for reasons unknown, one of the young women who Lido had dated was probably his undoing when she informed the Fascist police of his activities. Memoirs regarding his probable experiences in prison left no doubt as to the terrifying effect that internment would beget for any luckless captive, yet it didn't stop the Partisan attack.

****

Number 145, Via Tasso was situated on a remote Roman back street. All its windows were barricaded, and the décor was deceptively masked in modern color and design. Inside the building there were two wings; on one side the "offices," the other side the squalid prison.

A prisoner brought in was walked down a long corridor, at the end of which was a manned desk.

Seated behind it were two Fascist soldiers who after making several phone calls, gave the guard and his prisoner the order to walk up several flights of stairs. At each floor there was another desk and an armed soldier that would signal to continue the climb until at last, they reached the assigned floor where the prisoner and his guard would continue through a short corridor with a single light hanging from the ceiling. After entering a small, dark cell, one discerned a heated stench, the smell of men amassed for too long in a foul-smelling room without enough air and the presence of sweaty human beings that had been too close to each other. The cells were of different sizes and generally contained four to six people.

In a corner, at the height of 2 ½ meters, there was a hole where the air should have passed but didn't. There was inadequate space for the people who constantly bumped into each other, trying in some way to stretch out on the cold cement floor. After a few days one would only learn the time of day by the noises that came from far away and sounding like the first prison toilet noises of the morning. Minimum time was allowed for the toilet that was followed by the "meal," then the toilet of the afternoon and that of the evening. If one had to relieve himself at any other time of day or night, he or she would be forced to use the same container used for eating. Hunger was constant.

When a guard entered the cell, all the prisoners had to jump to their feet, and if anyone inadvertently touched the wall with their sleeved hand, the prisoner would be quickly cuffed by the guard.

Anyone at any time was subject to interrogation that would last from an hour to a few days. All came back badly beaten. Many unrecognizable, covered in blood, disfigured from the wounds and carried by the head and legs by two guards who would throw the broken man back into the cell.

His life almost at an end, Lido Duranti, along with other Partisan heroes, went through such prison procedures before his most certain death. Rarely were prisoners ever released.

Hostile officers would occasionally call the relatives of the prisoners to induce a prisoner to talk. Lido's father was called to the prison and taken to a room where his son was tied to a chair. The boorish inquisitors had ripped out his nails and teeth, his face a bloody mask. Upon seeing him, Lido's father told his son, "Lido, for God's sake, tell them whatever they want!"

Lido could probably have saved himself if he had responded positively to the officer's questions. No one outside the prison would have known if or what he said, but there was a choice he had previously made, a ceaseless battle to retain his integrity with his comrades. Lido coughed up blood and hoarsely whispered to his father through swollen lips, "What do you want me to tell them? I don't know anything!"

The nightmare continued for father and son. Maintaining a sworn oath that he knew would take him to his death, Partisan leader Lido, along with other heroes from the Via Tasso prison, were ultimately killed during the massacre at the Ardeatine.

Years afterward, the Italian Minister of Defense decorated the memory of the young man with the Silver Medal, its inscription reading:

> Fervent patriot Lido Durante started right after the armistice the fight against the oppressors, and performed in numerous, bold actions of sabotage. After the capture of four of his subordinates, disregarding the danger, he boldly surrounded the barracks where they were detained and liberated them. After being captured and imprisoned in Via Tasso, he stoically endured the tortures without betraying his companions, until, at the Fosse Ardeatine, with the ultimate sacrifice, he gave his life for the liberty of the country.

Lido was not alone in the fight. His Partisan brother, Nello, had been luckier. He lived to receive Italy's Military Cross for Valor after the war, which was inscribed with the following statement:

> As a commandant of a GAP formation he distinguished himself in numerous actions of guerilla warfare and sabotage. Captured by the Germans after a bitter fight, with courage and disregard of danger, he was able to escape from Infernetto where he had been restricted. He actively participated in the liberation of Rome.

Rome was finally declared an open city by Hitler's army before they retreated from American forces who seized it on June 4, 1944.

****

Months later, and 220 incredibly long kilometers to the north of Rome, the important city of Florence and its surrounding Tuscan villages still awaited liberation.

Municipalities such as Siena, Viterbo, Orvieto, San Gimignano and Montepulciano had to be taken before the Allied forces could reach the geographically significant Arno River bisecting Florence's renowned grandeur.

New Zealand's "Kiwi" troops had reached the south bank of the river as French and Moroccan soldiers were beating their way through Sienna. The battle-smoke had hardly cleared before the Germans declared Florence an open city, but playing for time to reinforce their tactical positions in Tuscany, they destroyed or impaired every bridge behind them that crossed the Arno except the historic Ponte Vecchio.

Sicilian born American OSS Major Max Corvo later related, "Florence was a city without water and food, and most inhabitants were trapped indoors. Long lines of men and women stood at a little dam crossing the Arno, and like a column of ants walked across to the south shore to pick up whatever meager food supplies were available. Occasionally, as the men and women carefully threaded their way across the dam, German shells abruptly brought their progress to a halt. The [U.S.] Army had set up water purification stations at various points throughout the city and lines of women bearing all sorts of receptacles stood patiently to gather the precious liquid and take it home."

Before leaving the city, and with full knowledge of their impending retreat towards the protective German Gothic Line, twenty kilometers to the north of Florence, the enemy massacred many administrative Italians known to be antagonistic to their cause, along with every captured Partisan.

Just before our American 91st Division could reach Florence, the attack shifted westward toward the important seaport of Leghorn and the mine-laden marshes and canals of Pisa's Marina. For weeks, our men fought fiercely for every inch of that well-defended Tuscan soil, and after taking Pisa, a few days of blessed R and R were sorely needed. Too soon, we were called upon again, this time, to penetrate the fearsome Gothic Line where Alberto and the rest of his Partisans joined us in the hellish mountain battle that began in September of 1944 and would last half of the longest year of my life.

The ensuing bitter winter would be long and hard but by early spring of 1945, the eminent city of Bologna had been waiting for us in the valley just beyond the last peak, terribly anxious to be free from their years of suppression.

A group of young Partisans.

CHAPTER FOUR

Partisan Women

I taly's general attitude towards women who enlisted in Partisan brigades altered gradually during the height of the country's 1943-1945 difficulties. In the war's earliest stages, most of the population believed women should stay home, cook and sew the clothing their men would need. That attitude changed as reports arrived about the few women who had joined Partisan groups, especially those who dared to act on their own, when word of their heroic actions and bravery under fire turned to admiration.

Austere associations of the "gentler sex" that had been slow to support their own gender had offered what they considered to be a practical alternative: "Do what you can, but provide the men with support, gather supplies and offer aid to the wounded." Yet, the numbers of highly motivated women who refused to stay home rather than fight continued to grow.

One of those with good cause to become active was Gina Borellini, who was later recorded as a recipient of Italy's Gold Medal for Military Valor. Her husband and brother were active Partisans and had been operating in the Modena resistance movement, where, at first, Gina carried out orders by transporting weapons and other imperative supplies.

Along with her husband, she had been arrested on several occasions by Fascist police but soon afterward released. He, however, was detained and finally shot.

After that tragedy her brother was imprisoned, impelling Gina to become even more active when she joined a local Partisan group. Documents about her exploits state that she suffered the loss of a leg in a battle against an overwhelming German force.

Carla Capponi had also left the comfort of her family's apartment. Hardheaded and tough, she lived on the run, often migrating to and from various areas near Rome, doing whatever was required to join the fight alongside a group of resistance fighters. Young, blonde-haired and attractive, Carla gradually assumed more weighty responsibilities and was ultimately promoted to vice commander of her squad, a title she earned by killing Germans.

Her first assignment had been the task of assassinating a Nazi officer as he left the Hotel Excelsior in Rome. The Partisans knew that he carried a briefcase filled with official papers of the city's important defense system. After shooting him and collecting the briefcase, Carla took flight through the drenching rain, dazed but gun still in hand.

She often slept on cold, dirty floors along with the male Partisans in her group, stressfully enduring what she described as "deplorably embarrassing experiences with the dozen or so male Partisans of my group." Inadequately dressed and poorly fed for the array of daring exploits she was credited with, Carla stoutly endured the loss of one of her lungs along with various malignant diseases resulting from her tenure as a Partisan commander.

Details of her transitional state after that first experience as an assassin reveal Carla's gratification during one of the more fortunate Partisan raids that ambushed and killed thirty-three of Goebel's hated S.S. men. That attack was followed with heinous enemy reprisals and the execution of the 335 Romans at the Ardeatine Caves, but she was extremely lucky to have escaped that certain death. Later in life, her characteristic response to the oft-asked question "Was it worth it?" was, "If I had to, I would gladly kill again every German I've already killed."

Continuation of Partisan actions had involved similarly in-clined, strong-minded women. During September of 1943, Italy's governing body had crumbled as confusion reigned in the capitol and the king's loyalist Army failed miserably in preventing the German occupation of Rome. Carla and a friend, Marisu Musu, were then an integral part of a central Resistance group that had participated. Undaunted and resolute, her cadre had grown and extended into a stronger network of zonal units that consisted of fifteen individuals of both sexes, their goal to make life in Rome hell for the Germans, and in which the two were uncommonly successful. Several other groups had a high female participation operating alongside Partisan forces where and whenever required, and the two dauntless women were later awarded Italy's Gold Medal "for decisive actions beyond the norm."

At the age of twenty, Edera de Giovanni had been working in the area of Bologna as a servant, but spent her spare time deliv-ering anti-fascist propaganda tracts.

Fresh groups of Partisans had begun to spring up everywhere, and when she heard about the organization of a new group of men and women near Rome, Edera enlisted. She severed her ties in Bologna and made her way over the Apennines to complete the 200 mile trek to the Eternal City to enroll. That group would be officially credited with disabling essential enemy telephone lines that ran from Rome to the Brenner Pass in the Alps, as well as to German headquarters in Berlin. After a year of assisting in and creating mayhem for her enemies, Edera and six others of her group were caught and arrested on March 6, 1944, and sum-marily executed.

In December, 1943, Novella Albertazzi had been a furrier in Bologna before joining the eighty women that had been part of the 200-member, 7th Partisan Brigade. Her devotion to work for the Resistance was made powerfully compelling by the loss of one of her brothers who had been shot and another imprisoned. It was said that she "fought like a man." Novella was wounded, arrested and later released. Almost immediately, she returned to the fight. Albertazzi, or "Vanda," her preferred Partisan sobriquet, led a unit of women stationed at their newly established base in Milan during a Partisan offensive when they were attacked by a strong Nazi regiment. Vanda's women held off the enemy's Mark IV tanks and artillery, turning their infantry away after a long and bitter fight. The women of her group would later go on to do battle in other troubled Emilia Romagna areas.

Male Partisans in the 7th Brigade were immensely impressed and openly displayed more and more admiration for their female soldiers as the war progressed.

The Germans had not yet left the battle zone below Rome when seventeen-year-old Maria Gaudino's dramatic action emphatically negated what had once been considered as the female stereotype. Maria had been on her way to get water at the fountain of the piazza in her small village when shots rang out around her. Having little knowledge of politics except for what the Fascists and Germans represented, she came to a quick decision to assist the Partisan recipients of the enemy gunfire, those she knew to be the village's Resistance fighters.

After picking up a rifle that had fallen when a nearby Partisan had been hit with a bullet, she was seen to have made good use of it. Maria had now become "one of them."

"I fired for more than two hours," she said. "I wanted to shoot them all. It had been a terrible year of bombings, hunger and thirst, and I became possessed with a great anger."

Another woman, Diana Sabbi, enlisted in the Resistance movement in the fall of 1943, joining two uncles who had been active Partisans in the city of Bologna. In June 1944, she joined the highly acclaimed Garibaldi Brigade, a considerable force of heroes who fought into the steep uplands of the Romagna mountain peaks. Those granite-faced mountains posed quite a challenge for her as she and her comrades were constantly on the move. With little or no supplies, and later in winter's bite of seasonal wind, sleet and fog, the brigade had lived mostly on chestnuts. Unhappy with the frigid surroundings, the brigade commander decided that they must move to another, more amenable area, and sent Diana to reconnoiter for a new location.

She had hiked the rocky slopes for a little over a mile when she heard a shout. Two German sentries had their guns leveled at Diana and her local guide, warning them to stop. Quick-witted and alert, she struck first and shot them both, then left the area as quickly as possible to avoid capture by an unseen garrison of enemy troops who were probably in the vicinity. After that frightening incident Diana had thoughts of turning back, but remembering the importance of her mission, she continued onward in another direction to complete her commander's assignment.

Another interpreted document relates to Rosanna Colleselli's special duties as a courier for the Partisan/OSS Aztec Mission in the mountains. Her stories relate what occurred along the area of the Piave River, flowing from the Alps towards the Adriatic Sea, not far from the city of Venice:

> At the end of 1944, the movement was reorganized into the Piave Area Command, which controlled an Information Service headed by Dr. Raffaele Da Val. A network of informers was set up, involving the locale's policemen who were either retired, on leave, or in active service. They were to report on the comings and goings, and general movement of the German troops. Other covert agents were operating in the town, some even

working within the German Administration itself. In the Police Headquarters several Italian Public Security agents kept me informed of any arrests, detainees and the state of the German morale.

My job was to piece together the information and convey it to my superior or directly to the mission leaders. I still possess some papers containing outlines of maps which the rapid course of events did not allow me to deliver to their destination.

I was already frequenting this group when, in November 1944, I began to work with Colleselli, later to become my husband, to organize the escape of Attilio Tissi, one of the leaders of our movement. Tissi had been arrested, tortured and detained at Gestapo headquarters. It was here, however, that one of our most valued informers was working as a driver: Rodolfo Dalvit (Sette), who came from the same village as Colleselli. Sette collaborated in every possible way with great courage, and not only on this occasion. He provided us with moulds for duplicating keys, the movement of the guards and plans of the premises. His cooperation allowed us to carry out a perfect plan of attack.

This was the background with which I officially entered the Information Service as their courier. My first contact with the Kappa Mission began with the meeting with Daulo Foscolo in Belluno's Piazza Campitello (now Martyr's Square), with a primrose as the sign of recognition!

In the meantime, there had been the "Clean-up Operations" of March 1945 and the mission had moved, stopping at my house in Praloran and crossing over to the right bank of the Piave River at Villa Tattara di Giamosa in Belluno. Villa Tattara had a very safe and well-hidden bunker where I went on an almost daily basis to deliver and receive correspondence.

At this point I will recount an extraordinary episode: One day our informer, Sette, warned me indirectly, through his brother, who often acted as a go-between, that the Germans had acquired a radio direction finder to ferret out any clandestine Partisan radios. There had been some imprecise signals coming from the right bank of the Piave and I headed straight towards Giamosa to warn them of the danger when I spotted a wagon with its antenna extended, slowly advancing down the road. I was on my bicycle, and naturally, I overtook it and rode quickly towards Villa Tattara where the members of the mission, in military dress as was their habit, were at ease playing the guitar! They were sure to handle that situation without problems, and I left.

In another episode, Daulo Foscolo told me one day, "Tomorrow I am going to Zoldo with Lieutenant Karl (head of the Gestapo) to make contact with the Partisans of the Val Cordevoli. (This was organized by our artful collaborator, Countess de Obligado.) Daulo requested that if he was not back before 6:00 p.m. to tell his sister Giuliana. Fortunately he returned in time that evening and I never spoke to anyone about the matter.

After another day I received an order from the 7th Alpini Brigade to meet the Countess in the square and keep ourselves busy until the men arrived who were to accompany her to the mountains. In this way I got to know that the heads of the Area Command of the meeting that had been attending a military tribunal had already met and that the Commander and Commissioner of the Val Cordevole had been summoned, and accused of deal-

ing with the enemy. I told my chief, who sent me to Be-
nucci: it was not easy to convince him to intervene.

I was under the impression that he was trying to stall,
but after a few hours he asked me to inform Area Command that he himself intended to preside over the pro-
ceedings. Upon crossing the Piave, he stopped for a while
at my house, where the Partisans were waiting to accompany him to Ceresera. The meeting was regarding a sus-
pended trial, the two leaders from Val Cordevole remained
unpunished, and the Countess free to return home. On
the 25th of April, when the fighting began in Limana,
with great loss of life, the town's priest organized a meeting between the Germans and the Partisans to draw up
the terms of surrender.

That meeting took place at Praloran on 27 April between the German captain, an Italian officer and several
Partisans from the 7th Brigade together with Major Be-
nucci. I remember it well: three hours of discussion
with the Germans who were hesitant to surrender, the
Partisans who were making a great deal of confusion
outside the Villa so as to appear to be in great numbers
(whilst in fact there were only a few at that point) and
finally well into the night after the surrender of the
Germans.

****

Partisans from the area of the Po Valley forwarded another heart-
rending tale about a young volunteer, Irma Bandiera, of their 1st
Brigade, who was born in 1915, during the height of the Fascist era
and grew up in well-to-do family surroundings. Although high on
the social ladder of the community, her parents did their best to
conceal their liberal political beliefs.

Those who remembered described her as being "a calm, happy and generous girl," and a "very sophisticated *signorina*."

Twenty-five-year-old Irma had been enjoying a life of ease before Mussolini joined Hitler to share in his avaricious take-over of Europe's peaceful countries. As the war continued, and without the knowledge of her parents, Irma began to keep company with youthful anti-fascists, socializing affably with her peers in homes and cafes.

Before long, she enrolled in the local GAP (Armed Partisan Group) as a courier and eventually graduated to more dangerous combatant activities. On August 7, 1944, she was returning home after having delivered a cache of arms to the Castelmaggiore base, nine miles north of Bologna and was captured carrying important ciphered documents.

Irma found herself in an intolerably desperate situation when she refused to offer her Fascist captors any information. Making matters worse, she was a female as well as a Partisan. She refused to inform on her comrades and disavowed all knowledge of their names and locations.

The commonly used procedure of alternating inquisitors began as their mind-bending torture continued endlessly, but Irma held fast to her silence. Despite every intolerable cruelty heaped on her she remained stoic and still did not bend.

Her tormenters finally ran out of patience. Other robust, hard-headed men had bowed to the excruciating pain she had been undergoing, but slender-bodied Irma never gave in due to her intense hatred for the Germans that only firmed the resolve not to give in.

She stared at them with scornful, tear-blurred eyes in defiance that, in the end, caused her frustrated torturers to blind her.

Irma was barely alive when on August 14, 1944, the tyrants cast her into a pick-up truck and dropped her worn, trembling body onto a sidewalk facing her parents' window. One of them barked at her, "Come on, give us some names. One name and you can go free. Your mother and father are here right behind this window and can take care of you."

Irma did not answer. They filled her inert body with machine-gun fire, and left the scene cursing.

After so many incidents in which women had become confirmed champions for the Partisan cause, the question of their value under battle conditions had become meaningless—a gone, but never-to-be forgotten issue.

CHAPTER FIVE

Angelina

Winter 1944: The war in Italy had come to a dead halt in early October. During the six months that followed, biting cold Alpine weather chilled both the Germans across the snow covered gorge and the remainder of our battalion's infantrymen. Outside of an occasional night patrol and blindly hurling mortar and artillery shells at each other, we could only wait out the freezing winter before our exit from the mountains and our next attack.

I had spent more than half of my time in the igloo (a name assigned to our battalion's ice-encrusted observation post) when our company's leathery First Sergeant, John O'Connor, felt sorry for my grievous condition and offered me a furlough.

Surprise! My hearth and home for the following eventful week was to be in a prearranged billet somewhere in Montecatini Terme, a warm and sunny Tuscan city thirty miles west of Florence. Wherever that strange sounding place was couldn't have mattered less to my burlap wrapped legs and frost bitten nose. I'd be crazy to refuse.

In my younger more cloistered life, I had never been aware of that world famous city that had been well known before the war as a favorite spa and trysting place for the rich and famous. Suddenly reenergized by what we saw when we arrived, the other fourteen khaki-clad foot-soldiers and I leaped off the canvas-

covered transport and rushed pell-mell into the warmth and activity of a bustling urban sprawl. The place appeared untroubled
and homey, peppered with close-packed tenements, shops and
the usual assortment of local pedestrians.

Having been well taught in directional map reading it was
easy to find my designated building, cop a quick glance at the
ten mail boxes and wrestle my duffle bag up to the next landing.
I gently thumped the knocker against door that would be my
next bedroom wondering who might be peeking at me through
the door's eyehole as I waited for a response. A minute passed. I
listened to sounds of a well-played piano that resonated pleasantly
through the doorway before I knocked again, louder this time.

The pianist's version of "Embraceable You" tapered off and
the door slowly opened to a scene that could easily have been
mistaken for a mirage. Before me stood a well-stacked, black-
haired beauty, framed like a pin-up starlet in the doorway of a
smartly furnished living room. Peering clumsily beyond her, I
was shocked to see two former associates of mine, Dean at the
piano, and Ron, toying with the reed of his clarinet. Both were
91st Division musicians with whom I had often shared the stage
as the band's vocalist back in the States.

It was apparent that military life had been good to them since
they had been stationed there during the months I had been freezing
my tail off in the mountains. I wasn't sure whether I envied or
hated them for enjoying such inordinate luxury, but especially for
having diverted themselves with their non-paying guest, Angelina.
I must have stood there for a full minute before unclenching my
jaw long enough to greet them. All three enjoyed my bewilderment
but seemed glad to see their stateside colleague.

I never would have expected anything like the scene I was
witnessing, especially after the agonies our men had been en-

countering in Italy's killing fields. Curiosity prodded me to first ask what in the hell was going on. Ron quickly informed me that our division's Special Service Company and its marching band had been spread throughout Montecatini, bunking in quarters similar to the three-bedroom flat I would share during my week's stay.

It was obvious that those two rakes who were a few years older and considerably more sophisticated than I, didn't give a hoot for anything as long as they could play their instruments and keep themselves in wine, women and song. Unaware of the raging battles that occurred so few miles from the action, how could they feel contrite? Who could blame them?

It seemed that the stunning, live-in *puttana* and her two sergeants had allowed me a furtive glimpse of a hedonistic side of life I never knew, and in a way, prepared me for some of the lascivious ways of the world I had yet to learn.

Sassy, ripe-mouthed Angelina, an unseemly name for a prostitute, was being kept very inexpensively. Beside the current roof over her head, all that the raven haired, hip-swaying enchantress seemed to require was three meals a day, a few pairs of nylon hose, cigarettes, chocolate bars and wine. For these simple things in life, she seemed likely as not to give her all and be allowed to live in the lap of luxury. Although generously offered to share in her charity, I never took advantage of it, and instead, became her friend.

Two days later I was jolted by an eye-opening discovery. The simple rewards for services rendered were not all that the lovely looking woman was capable of. Angie, as she requested I call her, was a loquacious sort, and more than generous in confiding her recent importance in the Partisan war of liberation. She evinced no sign of regret when she related how she had gotten into her profession at the age of fifteen. Even at that young age, she had been attractive enough to be seduced by an older cousin, and having enjoyed the experience, continued to use her feminine wiles to obtain sex freely until she left school a year later. It was then that a friend, Gina, advised her to sell what she had been giving away, and without remorse, Angie joined Gina as a call girl.

Four years later, Hitler's army of occupation had spread its troops throughout most the entire Italian peninsula. By then, German officers had learned to appropriate any commodity that appealed to them and assumed that tempting young women like Angelina were included. Some of the women had become impoverished, hungry enough to sleep with German soldiers mainly for the provisions they offered.

A number of those courtesans were caught sharing their beds with the Germans and summarily purged by vigilante teams of straitlaced, angry women who would then shave the harlot's head bare. Having exposed herself to a similar threat during the first year of sleeping with the enemy, Angie admitted to being extremely fearful of that shameful punishment and quickly learned how to manage and evade being captured by those who would be more than willing to remove her treasured locks. I had asked out of curiosity what means she took to escape that demeaning fate. Grinning sheepishly and, with a twinkle in her eyes, Angie explained, in her way, "It was simpler to shack up with Fascist landlords, or arrange a percentage of my take with hard-up barkeepers who didn't mind serving the fucking German officers. All kept hush-hush, you know, away from prying eyes. But, of course, I had to be damned careful."

Angie couldn't be accused of holding anything back, and what you read here is an artless translation from the unforgettable time we shared. Considering her diminished lifestyle, and with absolutely nothing to lose, she didn't have to disclose anything of her amazing past, but she did, for which I will be forever grateful. Angie unfolded bits and pieces of her turbulent, real-life experiences during my week's stay in Montecatini, and fortunately, she had learned a measure of English and German; I, enough Italian to comprehend her story.

Her involvement with the Partisans began one evening in the bar where her attractiveness captured the eye of a middle-aged German officer, Lieutenant Colonel Hess. Sitting alone at the next table, he had responded to her sly flirtation with an invitation to join him for a drink. She turned her chair to face him and Hess promptly assured her that language wouldn't be a problem since his mother was Roman and often spoken to him in that tongue.

Both engaged in the usual dallying games as he signaled the barkeeper to bring the entire bottle of cognac. They played touchy-feely for a time until he teased her with a proposition to come north with him to the plush seaside city of Santa Margherita Ligure, adding soothingly, "It isn't far from Montecatini, less than three hours by car."

Angie admitted that she had only been "playing the game" until he let it be known he'd be busy most of the time and would only be around on evenings he wasn't needed at his station. Her momentary silence assured him. He let it be known that he had been transferred from the front lines to take over a camp of new conscripts that would have to be quickly trained in the art of mountain fighting.

Soothingly persuasive, he won her over by promising that Angelina would have her own place to stay with sufficient money to spend any way she wished.

"Business was slow anyway, and so many of my clients had been forced to leave the city. Why refuse? Besides, it would be nice to stay at the beach for a while."

This from Angie as she looked to me for tacit approval. I agreed. Anything to keep her talking. Satisfied, she continued,

"Facing the sea was much grander than I expected. And it felt wonderful to be chauffeured around like a rich lady."

Hess had kept his promise. His driver delivered her and a minimum amount of luggage to an apartment near the seastrand visible from her third story window.

It pleased her that the colonel would be gone on most days, returning only on occasional evenings for sex and dinner. Every Italian woman in the world knew how to cook and she arranged her life to be on her own until he'd return to the apartment.

Gina, Angie's intimate friend and erstwhile business associate, had left Montecatini two months before her to be near her current beau, Mario. An important Resistance fighter, he too, often left for duty elsewhere while she remained in Rapallo, less than eight miles from where Angelina had taken up residence with Hess. Angie knew where Gina had moved and kept the telephone lines sizzling, comparing day-to-day notes with her friend like two high school girls. Never knowing when Mario would return, Gina hesitated to stray far from Rapallo. They had often shared their regular clients when they were home in Montecatini, sometimes doing "doubles" when their clients desired it.

When Gina left, Angie took on what remained of her friend's clientele, and those few additional tricks had sustained her in black market food and housing until she met Colonel Hess.

Gina had been sternly warned never to mention her connection to the Partisan cause. "Not to anyone! Not even your own family!" Mario had repeated emphatically.

Angie hadn't realized that her friend had an intimate relationship with the Partisans and only afterward learned that Mario had known of her move from Montecatini and had supplied Gina with Colonel Hess's background, telephone number and address. It frightened her to know that the Partisans were so vigilant.

Gina admitted to Angie that her instructions from Mario were to "Convince your friend, Angie, to help us," and following orders, she'd try.

At that time, Mario's Partisan group, along with others, had been active in the vicinity of the strategically important Via Aurelia Highway, a main thoroughfare used by the Germans to transport supplies between Rome and the Alps. With Angie's apartment in Santa Margherita so close to the highway's halfway point, she could certainly have been of immeasurable value to the Partisan cause, and the two friends would have to meet to gain Angie's cooperation.

Only a short distance away, Gina preferred to take the local bus rather than use the doubtful privacy of the phone when it came to secretive matters. Both agreed that a safer plan was to "accidentally" encounter each other in the bar that Angie began to frequent. "Just to be around people," she told me.

Local residents and homesick German soldiers frequented that cocktail lounge, allowing her to dress more conservatively than when she had to openly advertise her occupation. Indulging herself in the "not for sale" pleasures of time on her hands, she made sure those visits would be short, and convenient enough to make herself available near the hours her colonel was expected. Lovely of face and body as she was, Angelina couldn't help but attract attention wherever she went, yet it was obvious that she was bright enough to know where and when to put off possible suitors.

As yet an undetermined player in the resistance game, Angie couldn't have been aware that the Partisans had been observing her every move outside the apartment. Nor was she onto the undercover SS spy that had been keeping her in sight when she walked along the rocky shoreline or relaxed in the bar. It was natural for her to talk to the bartender or any woman she might

befriend, but men would be discouraged. She flatly rejected several attempts at the flirting game that would have been easy to
pursue. Why take the chance?

At that point in her story, Angie poured us both another healthy
shot of cherry brandy before continuing. "It still frightens me.
I'm sure he would have killed me if I dared do another trick."

Eleven days after she arrived in Santa Margherita, Angie had
been doing her usual walk along the strand when her friend suddenly surprised her. Gina had been waiting for Angie, sitting on
a bench among the large boulders that lined the town's craggy
shoreline. The two friends hugged and affectionately chattered
for forty minutes before Gina felt she could tell Angie the reason
for their clandestine meeting.

"We need your help," Gina pleaded.

"So tell me, who is *we* and what do you mean by help?"

Gina seemed uneasy and suggested that they go to a bar, needing a potent drink to help her explain. Once the mission to enlist
her to the Partisan cause had been revealed, Angie realized that
what Gina was asking could be a matter of life or death. They
both knew it and a hushed silence followed.

The bartender had been signaled by Angie for another round
of brandies during the unusual quiet as Gina glanced suspiciously
around the bar and asked, "Do you know these people? We can
go back to the beach if you think it's safer to talk there."

Angie's animated eyes peered around, studying the patrons.
Besides the few regulars she recognized, three unfamiliar loners
were sitting at the counter; none was talking to the bartender.

"Maybe we better go," Gina said. Angie had never seen her
friend so serious about anything before.

At the beach once more, the winter chill had drifted off the
Ligurean Sea, making their flesh bead into goose bumps, but
they felt free to speak normally since no one had followed them

out. Angie did most of the talking, asking relevant questions while Gina continued to press her.

"Our people need you, Angie. All they want you to do is remember who you and your friends are. If you hear anything, troop movements...any information that would help our cause... call me right away. And don't worry, I'll handle the rest."

Like most freedom loving Italians, Angie could not ignore the increasing resentment against Italy's enemies. Yes, she had slept with them, but that was different. Too many men she knew, Roman clients and relatives, had either been killed on an unnamed battlefield, or were hidden away in some foreboding prison. And when the colonel had no more use for her, she knew that picking up the pieces of her past wouldn't be easy.

At that moment, what Gina had requested didn't seem too dangerous, and well-meaning Angie promised that if anything important came up, she'd call.

November and December passed in a military stalemate. The colonel's attitude toward his whore had become relaxed to the point of showing her off to his staff. He began taking her to occasional social gatherings, and Angie admitted to enjoying that part of their relationship. She even said that traveling in style with the colonel in his chauffeured car "always made me hotter."

By February, Angie noticed that the colonel was becoming moodier, more morose.

The winter months were passing with little real news. She couldn't have understood that with the Russians taking a heavy toll on the Germans, Hess was being pressed to defend the Apennine Mountains from Partisan brigades with what the untrained riffraff had transferred from Berlin's subjugated territories. His libido had been suffering noticeably and Angie suspected he might have begun to tire of her. She finally summoned the courage to ask him why. His response was clipped, frightening her. "We'll talk later."

That was all he said before he rushed off to his encampment. When he returned that evening he was more solicitous, admitting his behavior wasn't due to anything she might have caused. His apologetic demeanor was unusually pleasant and Angie quietly waited for the other shoe to drop.

He sat down to his beaker full of imported schnapps, and quickly downing it, poured himself another before continuing. Hess had been slurring his words since he arrived later than usual at the apartment. Evidently, the man had already had more than a couple of drinks.

"I will have to leave soon," he muttered softly, apologetically, when suddenly his voice changed. "Damned Kesselring wants more fucking action! A counterattack, he wants! With what? Not enough manpower left in those damned mountains to even fight the fucking Partisans, let alone the Allies. Shit! Another damned load of raw, stupid replacements now is the last thing I need!"

Angie understood enough of both languages to feel his frustration and rubbed his sagging shoulders to calm him. She had known enough moody drunks in her young life to handle him as she had others. "But it worked," she said to me, adding a satisfied grin.

Hess downed the last dregs in his glass and continued to vent in a faltering version of Italian and German.

"My recruits will have to be trained and learn to fight in five lousy days and I will have to go with them this time. I'm sorry, my dear. I may be gone a long time."

The telephone rang, interrupting his apologetic outpouring. She knew the call could only be for him. Who would be calling her?

"Yes, this is Hess," he answered, muffling his previous anger.

From where she had been refilling his beaker, Angie could

hear but not make sense of the call. Several minutes passed while Hess listened, scribbling notes into a pocket pad, and obviously receiving important orders.

Responding stiffly, he repeated some of the words the voice on the other end had spoken.

"*Ja, ja*...will leave the area promptly at seven...rendezvous with you at Varese Ligure...Saturday. *Heil Hitler.*"

That part of the four-minute phone call over, Angie barely understood the implied drift of the rest of his communication, a word or two here, a number there. But even those few, obscure details might be important to the Partisans.

Angie had become unusually thoughtful before revealing to me that she had been awake a long time that last night with Hess, maturely considering who and what she was to this German colonel. "Nothing but a frivolous plaything to cater to his homesick penis. The bastard probably had a wife and kids at home he'd never tell me about, and if this would be my last week whoring myself to this man, fuck him! I knew I could always go back to Montecatini."

Hess left early the following morning and Angie nervously telephoned the number Gina had given her. The phone in Rapallo rang with no response.

Too keyed up to do anything else, she lingered restlessly in the flat for another few minutes, waiting to call again. This time a man's voice answered.

"Who is calling?" The coarse response startled her.

"Angie." She responded.

"Ah, yes," he replied. "Where are you calling from?"

"What fucking difference does it make—Santa Margherita! Is this Gina's number?"

For a moment the line went silent. She waited but the voice on the other end didn't reply. Annoyed and nervous, she asked again, "Is this Gina's number, yes or no?"

Whoever it was on the other end had hung up. Her flesh crawled with fear, this time concerned for her own safety. Angie knew how the German SS reacted to anyone who got in their way, and the thought of being stuck in some hellhole of a prison terrified her.

Even as she was relating the experience to me her voice faltered, her face turned pale and her shoulders shivered noticeably. After refilling our drinks she resumed from where she had stopped.

"I sat on the bed for a while and helped myself to his goddamned schnapps for another half hour until the ringing of the phone frightened me. It was the same man, this time he sounded a little nicer."

"My name is Mario. Don't talk now," he said. "I will meet you at the bar at twelve o'clock. noon. Please don't be late."

Angie couldn't respond since the line went dead after his last order.

"The man that called was definitely Italian, a good sign," she said, "and Gina's friends would never be fucking Fascists. A Fascist wouldn't have been so secretive, so cautious. Anyhow, I hadn't yet committed to anything that could incriminate me."

Around twenty to twelve, she sat at a table in an obscure corner of the bar and ordered a cognac, telling the amiable bartender that she would be waiting for a friend from out of town.

Twelve o'clock. A few customers had been drifting in, but one man, nondescriptly dressed and unshaven, headed in her direction. Before arriving at her table, he stopped partway to light a cigarette while his eyes took in the bar's patrons. She tensed as he plopped into the seat opposite her. The first words out of his mouth set her at ease.

"I would know you anywhere!"

After scouring the bar's patrons again he got up muttering, "Let's get out of here. Go someplace where we can talk."

Leaving most of her drink, she followed him in silence to the center of Santa Margherita's busy beachfront. Obviously, the man was in a hurry, didn't want to waste time with small talk. "Gina said you would phone when you had anything to report. What's up?"

"First, tell me who the hell you are".

Angie's phenomenal recollection of their meeting was surprising, leaving no doubt that she could have been much more than a prostitute had her life taken any other direction.

"It's enough to say I am an officer in the Centauro Division for our Via Aurelia Partisan group," Mario said. Thanking her for being cautious, he continued to explain that his was only a branch of a larger brigade that covered the entire Italian Riviera zone. "I suppose you want to know about Gina, yes? Why she isn't here?

He had hardly taken another breath before he went directly to the question Angie urgently waited for.

"We had to make a pick up in Genoa, a load of arms and ammunition that usually escaped the eyes of the Germans before being transported to Rapallo. With enough guns and bullets in that shipment, we could squeeze the bastards harder…rid ourselves of as many of them as we could before the Allied troops arrived.

"Gina was aboard one of those skiffs, but I'm sorry to tell you she didn't make it. When it landed near our hideaway, the fucking Nazis were there, waiting."

The last was a terrible blow and she couldn't hear anything further Mario said until he squeezed her hand as if to steel her for more. His head kept shifting as he peered around at the strollers before continuing.

"Had to be that some *Fascisti* son of a bitch had heard about our operation and told the Germans where our landing was going to be."

He turned to face her again, stating the obvious. "Angie, war is really hell. Some of us live, some die, but sweet Gina was caught in the middle. The bastards took a few prisoners, killed the rest on the spot. But we never found her body."

The seconds past quickly when he added, "You must have known that Gina was living with me in Rapallo...a wonderful woman. Hopefully, she is safe in a prison camp somewhere and will turn up when this damned war is over."

With that, he playfully placed his hand around Angie's waist, asking, "So, enough of me, pretty lady, what was your call about? Tell me, what was so damned important?"

It had taken less than a few minutes for Angie to absorb the alarming news that had come adjoined to Mario's brash forwardness: To her, it was a male's game of touch and feel that would end with a mute response of her acceptance. Angie said she had become used to that provocative device long ago, but the insolent gesture only intensified the worry of her own delicate position when and if she were to get involved with the Partisans. Her promise to Gina could not be ignored, especially now that her friend's fate might, in some way, be dependent on responding to Mario's question. Brushing off the boldness of his touch as natural, she told him about her colonel's phone call, the pending counterattack and Hess's frustration at having to depart the camp with inept reinforcements.

"Thank you, thank you so much," Mario said. "You don't know how much that information will help. Now we can *really* prepare for the bastards."

With that, he jumped up, kissed her surprisingly hard on her parted lips, then gave her another number to call if she could contribute any further details.

"Be careful, my dear," he added. "Our men in the area have been reporting on your colonel's activities, but we preferred to wait for the right moment. Your call gave us the answer we needed. Thank you, again. All Italy thanks you again!"

With that, he kissed her and furtively disappeared into a cluster of nearby pedestrians.

Angie's story had come to its dramatic close when her searching fingers rubbed my arm, asking once again if I cared to join her in the sack. I certainly could have, but remembering the prophylactic films the Army showed before we left the States, and a waiting young wife at home, I begged off. She smiled knowingly. An affectionate hug and kiss on the cheek would have to do.

I left Montecatini a few days later to return to my outfit knowing she'd be impossible to forget.

Five months later, our troops finally breached the last of Germany's mountain defenses. I wondered if the bloody battles that the Partisans were sharing with the Free World's troops had been mitigated by that one amiable *puttana*. I, and the world will never know.

****

Fifty-five years later I satisfied a yen to visit Rapallo with my wife and found it to be a charming, seaside town along Italy's lush Riviera. During a leisurely stroll into its wooded park that extends along the coastal side of that delightful hamlet I was poignantly reminded of Angie and Gina, and their valuable, unmentioned roles in neglected histories, when something incomprehensible lead me up the main path. I couldn't help notice a boulder off the path that had been inscribed with words honoring the brave, nameless Partisans that had been killed there. Wreaths

Roadside memorial dedicated to Italian Partisans executed on this spot by firing squad.
Located near Rapallo, in northern Italy.

and draped pennants concealed part of the inscription, but the
reminiscent loneliness of that haunting stone shrine will remain
with me forever (*see photo above*).

Many of us who participated in the Italian Campaign might
never have enjoyed the prosaic life we led afterward had it not
been for the Partisans and the extraordinary likes of the two
bold-spirited and engaging *puttanellas*.

CHAPTER SIX

The Tuscan Riviera and the Mountains to the North

The Time: Winter 1943 to spring 1944.

The Location: Tuscany's northwest coast and the nearby mountains.

The Situation: Ineptitude of the country's politicians and a general breakdown of morale prompted the rise of growing Partisan resistance in the north.. Shepherds and indigenous inhabitants living throughout the uplands knew the area well, and they, the hearty northern drudges, provided the cunning resourcefulness of the growing Partisan army. That cadre of unlikely heroes would become a force that would lead to the enemy's undoing.

A t the beginning of a report titled "Tuscany and the Gothic Line," the Italian Minister of Defense, Lelio Lagorio, offered the following reason for the increase of Partisan recruits:

> Someone had said that from the ashes of the old army, the liberation movement was born. We do not know if this is the right image but certainly in that period in the midst of so much misfortune, the first fully demanding

resolutions of armed battle for freedom were established. Much merit for this goes to those who had left the ranks of the scattered Italian Armed Forces.

The process of transformation of those fugitive soldiers into freedom fighters is undoubtedly one of the most fascinating chapters in our history.

Meanwhile, the safe comfort and unbounded solidarity of the greater part of the population towards those humiliated and persecuted soldiers is a fact that reveals the width and depth of the humane feeling that allowed so many of them to find the best part of themselves once more. Wide convergence of thought was established among those, and it was discovered that there were many who had motives for a meeting to coordinate their commitment to do battle, both in view of immediate and of working out more ambitious programs of wider scope. All this happened simultaneously and in a more obvious form in Tuscany, where there was a certain predisposition for this phenomenon.

****

On the northern edges of Tuscany, and only a few miles from the base of the Apuan Alps, the cities of Pisa and Lucca carried the major burden of oppressive Fascist *carabinieri* and German occupation troops.

As from other cities and villages near the Ligurian Sea, Tuscan cadres of civilian freedom fighters came forward, hoping to contact larger, more experienced groups, located near Florence, Viareggio and Grosseto to coordinate their guerilla operations.

Ruggero Parenti (Romeo), whose reputation as a leader among Partisans was legendary, had arrived in Pisa from his base of operations in Florence. Under his command a number of sabotage

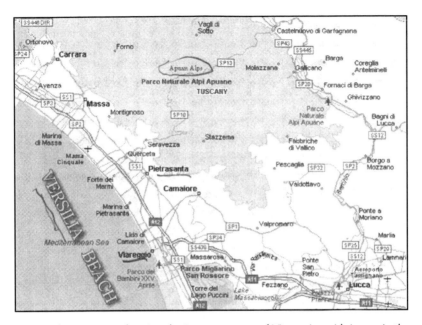

Apuan alpine region showing the important port of Viareggio, with Lucca in the southeast.

activities were conducted, particularly targeting the vital railways between Pisa-Firenze, Lucca-Pisa, Pontadera-Pisa and Pisa-Calci. Trains were derailed, others forcibly prevented from delivering German supplies and reinforcements.

In November 1943, Romeo's Partisans accepted assistance from a newly formed subdivision, "The Women's Group of Defense," consisting of female volunteers similar to those previously noted. Women of all ages contributed, acting as dispatchers, spies and dauntless warriors when required. These women often joined their male Partisan combatants in numerous clandestine operations as well.

By then, large numbers from former Italian Army forces appeared in the northern villages and mountain passes, where many

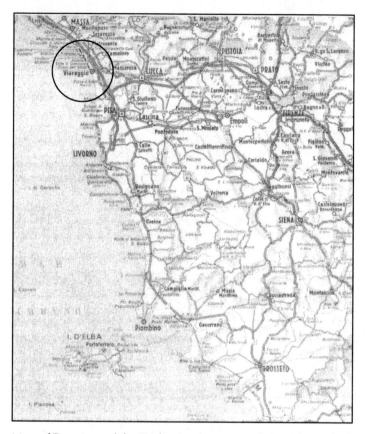

Most of Tuscany and the Tyrrhenian Sea coast, where cities and villages were fought for and eventually emancipated inch by inch. The Tuscan Riviera begins just north of Viareggio.

developed into outstanding freedom fighters.

Those invigorated cadres quickly matured into a homogenized legion of resistance groups, and their self-contained vigilante manner of unconventional fighting began to evolve into larger scale brigades that often numbered into the hundreds.

During this time, a large number of Allied soldiers had by one way or another made their escape from German captivity.

They had served in regiments that emanated from a profusion of countries that included Britain, America, France, Canada, South Africa, India, Australia, Tunisia, Morocco, Arabia, Poland, Palestine, the Boers, Italy and Yugoslavia. Very often those who managed to evade their captors chose to remain and join with resistance fighters in Italy's rugged upland.

Fifty-two Yugoslav Partisans had managed to break out of the area's Fascist prison just before Italy's northernmost area had been completely occupied by the Germans and remained to wander as refugees along the mountainous alpine promontories. Thirty-seven of that group ultimately crossed over the mountains towards their homeland, while fifteen still remained hidden and protected by local Tuscan peasants.

"These ex-prisoners were a great worry to our organization," wrote Ruggero Parenti, and a deep regret was felt at not being able to do more for the greater part of those men, some of whom were to be numbered among the ranks of the Pisan Resistance till war's end.

Uncountable military prisoners had made a run for it after taking flight from the Laterina POW camp, in the vicinity of Arezzo, fifty miles S.E. of Florence, and scattered in differing directions. Italian, Slav and Allied escapees remained hidden in farms near Arezzo where they found food, shelter and transportation that included all manner of assistance and occasionally the gift of money.

Thirty-three Allied ex-prisoners had covertly settled into the Convent of the Camaldoli Fathers, a list that had surprisingly included seven generals.

A number of them had been sent to Arezzo by the Partisan Florence Committee, with a recommendation that helped them reach southern Italy and re-enter the Allied armies.

Even as their flight was being organized, the escaping men

German antitank ditch along the Gothic Line.

knew that German troops were marching towards Arezzo, and that the entire area would soon come under enemy control.

A Fascist sympathizer had discerned that several British ex-prisoners were hiding in the convent with the Camaldoli friars. He passed the information to the local German commander who ordered the local police to round them up. Although he agreed to carry out the request, the Italian police chief secretly sent one of his marshals ahead on motorbike to alert the Camaldoli friars before acting on the order. This allowed the English fugitives enough time to take flight.

As far back as March of 1942, anti-fascist graffiti had begun to appear on the walls of Pisa, usually with waggish phrases regarding Mussolini, Hitler and their local regime. Young people passed out anti-fascist tracts to women in market places, inviting them to join in protest demonstrations outside the Fascist feder-

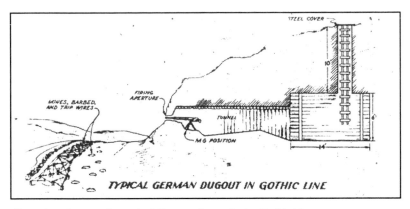

Illustration showing the typical German dugout in the Gothic Line.

ation building. One young woman, Lina, seized a small truck that delivered bread to Fascist headquarters and light heartedly distributed its wares to the onlookers until a German guard pointed his rifle at her, ready to fire. A bystander, Ugo Camerata, hit the guard with his fist. Two other Germans began to fire but Ugo managed to dodge their wild fusillade that was cleverly averted by the boisterous interference from women who were marketing.

After that unprecedented act, groups of young Pisans began to intensify their rebellious uprisings by gathering arms and ammunition, the beginnings of a hoard of weapons covertly confiscated from a local Fascist military warehouse.

On September 20, 1943, Gino Lombardi and his Partisan group struck. Dressed as a police brigadier, he presented himself as a Fascist, enabling his men to confiscate much of the local Blackshirt ordnance and transported it to a secret location in the hills above Pisa.

Another group led by Valentino Orsini and Fidio Bartalini had also seized a mass of arms from enemy barracks, adding insult to injury by disarming several German trucks traveling along the Aurelian highway. A large part of their captured arms and ammunition were sent to Partisan formations battling the Germans in the nearby mountains.

Day by day the cautious attitude of Partisan groups active near the Apuan Alps became rashly bolder in their combat activities. In November and December 1943, the railway line between San Giuliano and Terme-Lucca would often be disrupted with the use of explosives, while far to the north, the well-traveled Brenner Pass highway in Emilia Romagna was sprinkled with tri-pronged booby traps placed in the roads. During that same time, Partisan Nardino Barsotti was given the task of transporting arms in the area of Montemagno di Camaiore (near Lucca) by disguising himself as a baker driving a small delivery van.

In January 1944, the same Barsotti, with the cooperation of friendly laborers, severely damaged four large enemy bunkers along the enemy's Gothic Line. He was caught and interrogated, badly beaten and tortured, but refused to reveal the names of his Partisan companions before being killed.

The following descriptive incidents were acquired from Pisa's records and submitted in their characteristically brief format from one of the most active Partisan districts in the country:

> On January 3, 1944, a Partisan group in the vicinity a farming village were armed with handguns and hunting rifles when they were attacked by a small section of Fascist carabinieri. In the brief battle, one carabinieri was killed. The following day this same Partisan group, headed by Captain Mario Chirici, decided to join a larger group in the locality of Frassine. Together, their wide-ranging group successfully completed a large number of destructive actions against German and Fascist patrols.

On January 15, 1944, during a search operated by sections of the German SS, there was a violent conflict with the Partisans. Two Germans were killed and a truckload of enemy militia was set afire. One Italian Fascist was wounded.

On January 18, 1944, a group of Partisans severed the telephone line of the Prato-Boccheggiano stretch. On the 30th, on the roadway to Follonia, a German truck was set afire. On the 5th of February, the main telephone line in the zone of Massa Marittima was severed, while on the 12th, a truck on the roadway to Follonica was set on fire. One German was killed.

As a result of these continuous guerrilla acts, on the 16th Nazi-Fascists forces attacked groups of the Partisan formation positioned in Poggio Bocchini and Campo Albizi. In spite of their strong defense, five Partisans, Silvano Benedici, Pio Fidanzi, Otello Gattoli, Salvatore Mancuso and Remo Meoni were wounded by the Nazi-Fascists, then killed by repeatedly stabbing their bodies. The Partisan Otello threw his last hand grenade against the Fascists before being killed.

In nearby Val d'Orcia, in 1943, former Allied prisoners turned up at various houses in little groups to ask their way south, get some food and then go on their separate ways.

Although aware of the risk to themselves, most of the farmers were eager to shelter and help them. Many of those convicts had obtained and changed to civilian clothing, despite the risk of being shot as spies.

Whole villages not far from Arezzo became centers of assistance to the escapees. The town of Lucignano became a known

transit center for ex-prisoners, Italian fugitive soldiers and persecuted Jews headed for Vitiana, in the vicinity of Lucca. From
there they made their way to Monti di Villa.. Every evening,
more than two hundred refugees found lodgings there, and to
all, the population offered food and clothing.

The aid and assistance organizer in that area was Bruno Stefani,
a Partisan of undaunted courage. Partisan Giorgio Di Ricco wrote
that no one was a better scout, a more precise informer and a
more courageous courier than Bruno. "When he was finally captured and tortured," Di Ricco explained, "his devotion to those
persecuted by Fascism allowed him the rare opportunity to be
taken in front of his mother where he was heard to say, 'Mama
don't cry, I die for a just cause.'"

Many heroes like rancher Don Pasquino Borghi were charged
with having fed the atmosphere of insurrection with support and
hospitality they offered those errant bands of escapees. Borghi
was apprehended and killed after distinguishing himself to the
community as being helpful to wayfaring newcomers. Before he
was shot, he was placed stark naked in a public square and intentionally humiliated by the Germans. They had reasoned he
would receive the village's scorn, as well fear of receiving similar
treatment, but his death never altered the desire to continue their
covert aid to Allied bands of escaped wanderers, caring for them
as if they, too, were Partisan resistance fighters.

Winston Churchill wrote, "Out of the thousands of these men,
conspicuously clothed in battle dress, and in the main with little
knowledge of the language of the distant country, at least ten
thousand Allied servicemen were helped by the local population
and guided to safety, thanks to the risks taken by members of the
Italian Resistance and the people of the countryside."

It was noted that out of the enormous number of prisoners-of-war
held in enemy camps in 1943, almost half turned up safe in April

1945 and returned to their homes. Several thousand more had been able to return to the Allied lines or sanctuary in Switzerland.

The social and historical dimension of this operation was not lost on those who had fearfully waited for their loved ones at home. Not one of these escapes would have been conceived without the self-sacrifice and cooperation of many rural Italians; peasants, shepherds and old women, tough as the soil they tilled. The names of most are lost to history, but the generation that lived through that time can never forget their undying heroism.

Lelio Lagorio, who would later mature into Italy's Minister of Defense, became one of the brigade commanders, and with reports from commanders of the Garibaldi 4th Apuan Brigade, he set out the following anecdotal narrative regarding initial Partisan actions in the area of Grosseto:

> Straightaway, we decided to start offensive and sabotage maneuvers, as well as to intensify propaganda so that fresh, young recruits could become integrated. As a result, the group was becoming over-numerous and had reached the strength of almost two hundred men. It was decided to create a main nucleus, consisting of about seventy men, one of which was under the command of myself, while other bands were detached and acted in the nearby territory.
>
> We are on the borders of Emilia, in the area of the Apennine passes. Before 8 September 1943, a large detachment of the Alpini (Italian mountain troops under Mussolini's control at the time) was in the area of Cerreto Pass. Somehow, a suicidal fixation had invaded our Partisan unit; throw away your arms, your kitbags and go back to your homes.
>
> After the Alpini came the Germans, whose first care

was to organize a search for Partisan arms and equipment. In and out of the Partisan ranks the enemy crept unseen, dressed as coal-miners, shepherds, youths of little importance, mountain men from Sassalbo and Mommio. They took what they could; rifles found abandoned in the shrubbery, bayonets, ammunition, hand-grenades and a load of 75mm projectiles.

The TNT in these projectiles would later be recovered by Partisan Nuvlon, an artist and artillery officer previously freed from forced internment, and will be used in the first acts of (Partisan) sabotage. Tent canvas, along with worn German military jackets, all was hidden with the traditional astuteness of these Fascists but soon discovered by our men. Even mules that would prove useful to the Partisans, were taken away from under the noses of the Germans under cover of the night.

This early activity was not without its dangers and had its victims; some Partisans still carry splinters in their bodies from enemy hand-grenades.

Towns like Pisa and Leghorn [known as Livorno to the Italians and Lagorio's home town], torn to pieces by the ferocious aerial bombing of the Anglo-Americans, fell into line in the fight against Nazi-Fascists from terrible living conditions, at the limits of survival. The Duce's son-in-law, Galeazzo Ciano, had also become aware of and worried about the new reality of Leghorn, his town for some time.

Even Pisa had to wage its own war and appeared more like a graveyard than a city with scenes of the Apocalypse; twisted tramlines that sink into the ground and rise to the sky like dead snakes, carriages on their backs or on top of each other, contorted pylons, knotted cables and wires. The houses, along the sides of the railway, stared back with the black eyes of thousands and thousands of empty, broken windows.

****

Twenty miles north of Pisa, in unpretentious villages and districts like Pietrasanta, Ruosina, Seravezza and Forte di Marmi, freedom fighter volunteers sought and found one another. Once coalesced into groups, they would make contact with other battle-toughened brigades that had been centered near larger cities such as Lucca and Viareggio.

Gino Lombardi of Ruosina (a province of Lucca) gathered his small band of volunteers from Viareggio, a Ligurian seafront town situated along the important Aurelian Highway that wended its way northward from southern Italy. As a strategic thoroughfare it was mainly used to carry enemy traffic to north and south destinations near the country's Riviera coast.

With the appearance of zealous, Italian Partisans that had begun to impede their re-supply trips, German drivers could only travel at their own risk. Gino had been in radio contact with committees of the National Liberation Front in Carrara, and Special British Corps agents that had previously parachuted into his area. Through terse, coded transmissions, his group had begun to send and receive information and supplies from Allied task forces. Gino's select cadre of hand-picked fledglings assembled with other nearby splinter groups in the vicinity of Viareggio to commence their first aggressive action to filch a sorely needed cyclostyle copier that was needed for intercommunications. His group surprised the Fascists controlling the city hall in Seravezza when they invaded the building and hijacked the machine. That seemingly small incident boosted the area's Partisan spirits and would be the beginning of future significant operations by his men.

He was soon joined by other important patriots, like Luigi Salvatori of Pietrasanta and Manfredo Berrtini of Viareggio, who assisted Gino in the organization of his Partisans. Bertini's initiative on September 17, 1943, was materially aided by enlisting a courageous woman, Vera Vassalle. She was given the dangerous task of crossing enemy lines to contact Allied forces for the purpose of acquiring additional arms and information needed to expand the Partisan operations.

Conjoined forces in the area named themselves the S.A.P. (Squadredi Azione Patriottica) and busied themselves by expropriating armaments; flame throwers, machine guns, Berretta tommy-guns, rifles and all types of explosives from lightly patrolled German and Fascist ammunition dumps near Viareggio, Pietrasanta, Pisa and Massarosa. Those captured supplies were then stored in prearranged locations, sometimes with great difficulty in the wintry ice and snow covering the mountains in October. They would make use of them at a later time as they awaited more favorable fighting conditions.

The Partisan radio and its protective personnel had to be on the move after each broadcast for fear of German triangulation, a signal finding location system that the enemy almost always used to great advantage. Nevertheless, Radio-Azzari (a Partisan appellation) would often supply Allied pilots with valuable information regarding German troop locations by using disarranged code words such as "*Le sirene fischiano*" (the sirens whistle), and "*Per chi non credi*" (for whom that does not believe).

February 18, 1944. At 4:00 a.m., a British Halifax airdropped seventeen barrels containing fifty Sten submachine guns and necessary ammunition, sabotage weapons for hand-to-hand fighting, shoes and clothing. The field recovery of those sorely needed supplies had been accomplished by fourteen of the younger Partisans, including six who later died in battle. Even with all the precautions taken, the propitious launch was observed by nearby Nazi-Fascist police who set off the first chain of repressive attacks against the area's Partisans. The following graphic battle reports were acquired from Viareggio Partisans and translated into English:

February 25, 1944. In Forte Dei Marmi, almost the entire Partisan group called "Front of Youth" was arrested, but they had already accomplished much in the way of distributing propaganda and gathering arms, ammunition and sabotage.

On February 28, the hated Fascist chief of Forte dei Marmi, Colonel Gasperetti, organized an assault upon the home of Gino Lombardi. The break-in did not accomplish what was desired because Gino and his companion, Piero Consani, were able to escape. Gino took refuge at Porta di Farnocchia where he had established a base and a center of collected arms that gave life to the first formation of mountain Partisans, to which he gave the name "Cacciatori delle Alpi" (Hunters of the Alps). The problems were serious, especially the lack of food for a military formation on the heights of the Apuane Alps. Because of these problems only his action could save the preservation of the besieged Partisans.

Lombardi knew very well that in the brief period of his actions for the Partisan formation, he showed to have understood the principle of the patriot's fight, giving enthusiasm to all the population that resided near the Apuane Alps.

The Cacciatori delle Alpi Partisans grew stronger by obtaining additional men and arms. Some sailors from nearby Pietrasanta had deserted their ship to join the Partisans. On March 3rd the Partisans took successful action against a local *carabinieri* barracks to free some prisoners and to obtain arms.

On March 23,1944, because of danger of a roundup, Gino Lombardi's men, instead of hiding in other places, descended into the valley, requisitioned a bus and traveled to Arni. Even in Tambura, his Cacciatori engaged the enemy soldiers that had surrounded them. Lombardi was able to break the encirclement and return to Porta di Farnocchia. Because of the food problem, the Cacciatori broke into the cooperative of Ponte Stazzemese and confiscated all the foodstuffs.

Due to the constant troublesome activity of the Partisans, the province's Fascist chief, ill-famed Mario Piazzesi, decided to take action against the Cacciatori. On the 16th of April, 1944, his soldiers arrested Lombardi's family, including his fiancé, then burned his house.

At dawn of the next day, some hundreds of Fascist soldiers attacked the Partisans who defended themselves with valor, killing many of the assailants even though they had been superior in men and arms. The Partisans were able to break the attack. In this fight, twenty-year-old Luigi Mulargia from Sardinia died heroically.

The insurgent's Military Committee of Viareggio, in agreement with Lombardi, decided to transfer the Partisans from the Apuan Alps to the zone of Alta Lugiana, a more favorable place, and also for the ability to have direct contact with the Allied Command through Radio-Azzari.

On April 21st, Gino Lombardi, Piero Consani and Second Lieutenant of Infantry Otterino Balestri left Pietrasanta to go to Equi Terme to discuss the transfer of the men with Azziri. In Sarzana they were stopped by two Fascist soldiers and taken to the barracks to explain their positions. In the attempt to escape their capture, Lombardi, after killing a few Fascists, was himself killed. Balestri was able to escape but Consani was taken prisoner and killed at dawn on April 4, 1944.

****

Two months had passed, a time when my regiment had been battering its way towards Pisa and Leghorn, as yet unaware that Partisans were active in and around those cities. One of their noteworthy incidents came to my attention months later, when Alberto related the story of two friends who had recently returned from a small village, Massarosa, near Viareggio.

On temporary leave from their Partisan group, Frederico and Cesare had been planning a spur-of-the-moment act of sabotage that had presented itself inadvertently. Still in their late forties, they had disguised themselves to resemble aged, arthritic men. Cesare's clothes appeared to be in disrepair and he avoided being noticed by using makeup and a cane that made him appear feeble and lame.

Frederico, in contrast to his friend, donned a shaggy beard and wobbled unsteadily at his friend's side. Adding to his affectation, he appeared to support himself on Cesare's free elbow as if he, too, ailed.

It was Sunday and they had joined with other villagers, parents and children who were strolling the cobblestone streets towards early mass. With no transportation available, young and old alike had left their homes and approached the town's church in family clusters.

The two men intermixed their false frail bodies with the procession as they passed a hastily erected German military supply zone that was surrounded by a quadrangle of barbed wire. No larger than a football field, it made do for a temporary garrison for their transient soldiers who were stationed in the town. The

stockade had been avoided by the locals, but the town's sympathetic collaborators saw to it that its fronting street would be
busier than normal that Sunday.

The quadrant's main entrance was protected with two ma-
chine-gunners who watched the scene from raised platforms at
each side, while another two sentries paced the interior of the
makeshift fence. Its personnel garrison consisted of six camouflaged barracks tents, a grassy parade ground and a motor pool
area for vehicles of every type that seemed to be constantly on
the move.

Frederico had noticed that the lot was busier than usual on the
previous day and five tarp-covered transport trucks had lined up,
side by side, each of their tempting tailgates pressed close to the
garrison's rear fence.

At the opposite, main gated side, the guarded enclosure faced
the street that was speciously crowded with many parishioners
headed to church that morning. How long the trucks would
remain in their present position close to the barbed wire fence
could only be ardently invoked in their prayers.

With the next day being Sunday, and probably a slow day for
the garrison, the opportunity to incapacitate those trucks was one
that the two Partisans could not overlook. Yet, having previously
witnessed the sight of butcher-hooked Partisan comrades dangling
in the wind after capture, that memory could have easily led them
away from attempting the mad gamble they were considering.

In the end, they concluded that it would be the best way to
avenge their lost, fellow freedom fighters. The small town's sup-
portive network would then communicate with other villagers
who could be counted on but they would have to be sensitive to
the presence of Fascist sympathizers and avoid the possibility of
phone interception.

Word spread rapidly through the close-knit neighborhood,

carefully limited to known intimates only. Those who had chosen their road to the church agreed to bring their entire family along in order to bloat that route with as many people as possible. All that was needed to complete the plan arrived that evening in the person of a younger Partisan who resided in the town. Twenty-six-year-old Aldo worked as a baker's helper whose special task tomorrow would be extremely critical. After checking out three other recommendations, he seemed the most likely to handle the tricky task given him.

Frederico and Cesare couldn't have been more pleased when they saw the Sunday morning turnout, and the threatening sky didn't seem to slow anyone from attending church. The two Partisans were ready, and any thought of failure was far from their minds.

Nearing the entrance, Cesare's feet left from under him, his cane twisting underneath his full-bodied torso as he hit the ground. A crowd gathered to see what was happening as Frederico faked a desperate effort by trying to lift him. The nearest German machine-gunner attempted to maintain order from behind the barbed wire, shouting in German for the gawking crowd to stand back and away from the gate. From his position midway from the scene, an innermost sentry moved closer to gape at the scene in which a number of townspeople were slowly attempting to assist the fallen man from the sidewalk

Meanwhile, the third unnoticed Partisan, Aldo, furtively made his way through a tree-lined back street until he neared the scrubby, dirt-filled path outside the rear fence. As planned, an accomplice's ambulance with sirens shrieking complicated the scene as the wrist of the unseen Partisan's hard-gloved hand reached far enough through the fence's barbed wire grill to place several timed explosives under the tailgates of the trucks

By then, Cesare had successfully found his feet again and the street had almost been cleared of its bystanders as he slowly limped in the direction of the church. All this while, Frederico shuffled through the crowd, back to his waiting family.

There would be no rush since the town's collaborators had all been alerted to the explosive's timers that were set for 3:00 p.m. Enough time afterward for everyone to have settled down out of range.

By 1:30, four of the enemy's trucks had dispersed to carry their share of reinforcements and a load of supplies meant for their front lines. The single truck that remained in the compound did explode Sunday afternoon. No one from Massarosa could be seen near the quadrant during that time. The trucks that had left the compound were many miles away at the time, most likely spraying bursting shards of fiery ordinance and Nazi personnel into peaceful vineyards and mustard fields somewhere along the roads to the mountains in northern Tuscany.

CHAPTER SEVEN

Incident at Milan

The long awaited order to break camp had finally come, and with the Gothic Line behind us we'd be leaving our line of departure at the crack of dawn. Our generals had calculated that by storming the broad Po Valley ahead, we might catch the Germans unprepared for the level miles of open wheat and rice fields to our front. The three-year chase could end before they had a chance to reach the Alps. All of us were anxious to get the damned war over with and it would have been great if it could only have been that simple.

Still staring at us defiantly were thirty miles of stony peaks and sheer escarpments from where we'd have to dislodge the hard-nosed enemy before reaching our goal—the city of Bologna.

First, we'd have to get around and over Mt. Adone, Mt. Frati, M. Castellazzo, C. Boschi and S. Benedetto—steep crests that still concealed minefields, camouflaged artillery and well dug-in enemy machinegun nests. The last remnants of winter we'd spend in those Gates of Hell had not yet been concluded, and realistically, no one dared underestimate the potential of the Germans.

My friend Alberto and his Partisan comrades had left us sometime during the previous night, and as usual, had been scrapping somewhere in the mountains we faced. They would remain incommunicado until we reached the last of the downhill slopes before the Po Valley. Other Partisan groups that were east, west

Allied advance lines in the Po Valley and dates of previous battle lines in Italy, 15 January 1945, as they neared Milan. Map prepared by the Department of the Army.

and north of us had already extended their incisive forces throughout the sun-drenched valley, even having reached as far as the Austrian and French borders that became the razor-peaked Dolomites we dreaded.

After rejoining our company near Bologna, Alberto related another incident that had occurred in busy Milan, an incident that led to the narrow escape of his Partisan associate, Raffaele Rinaldi. The group had previously drawn straws for the "honor of destroying" Gino's Trattoria and Rafaele had won the polemic prize.

Gino, a restaurant proprietor, had died of a heart attack a month earlier, and left his elderly widow the neighborhood business. At that time brigades of Hitler's minimized minions were still stationed in the city and intended to remain there as long as possible.

Rosario, a brazen Italian police commander, saw an easy financial opportunity by ignoring the rightful protocol of the man's widow. He willfully assumed control of the business and deviously replaced the semblance of ownership, discharging the waiters and cooks. Then he arranged for a Fascist family of his own choosing to continue its operation, which would be made to appear as if they were the new owners.

The unscrupulous commander made sure that the restaurant was kept busily occupied as he slyly guided other officers and their aides to attend, craftily tending recommendations. Gino's wife complained to the city administrators but could do little to avoid being ignored by fascistic clerical personnel. Although her customers slowly began to avoid the confiscated restaurant, all went well for Commander Rosario as he collected his tax-free share of the lira.

It wasn't long before Gino's Partisan friends would see through the commander's scheme, and bitterly incensed, decided to put an end to the mischief that seemed hopeless. Before taking action, they were assured by friendly council that Gino had left enough life insurance to cover his wife for a long time. Now, without concern for the widow, they could be free to "hit it" after a payday, when it was likely to be filled with German officers and the commander's Fascist cronies.

In the uniform of a German lieutenant, Partisan Raffaele left a package and briefcase in the men's toilet. One of the timed devices detonated prematurely but luck was with him that night as he barely made his getaway from the heavy-set sentinel posted under the entry's canopy.

The blast and fire that followed the bombing killed twenty-seven of the enemy, but a few Blackshirt *carabiniere* near the front took up the chase.

The adventures that befell the Partisan in his flight that evening have been translated from Alberto's words, into what would have been Raffaele's more prosaic description:

I ran like the wind and found a nearby shell of a building that had been bombed out in an earlier Allied air raid. It was dark and my pants caught in the broken beams. Gravel and stones lacerated my hands and knees as I tried to crawl as far away as possible from the street. A hail of gunshots followed wildly into the darkness but missed me. The combination of cold air, anxiety and stress made me feverish.

Curfew time had just come and vehicles whizzed by with their sirens screeching. I had no choice but to force myself to lie flat on my stomach, pressing my head against the filthy rubble to avoid being caught in the beam of the headlights. Soon silence and threatening shadows returned. A cold mist had penetrated my bones and I felt miserable, scared. I had to get out of there, but how? I'd have to wait until later when it was safe.

About twenty minutes later a passing drunkard came
out of nowhere and made his way towards where I lay
and fell asleep into a snoring heap nearby.

Time passed. The street remained busy with police
and occasional pedestrians. The traffic rushed by, their
drivers glad to avoid the chaotic scene.

My drunkard companion snorted and snored inces-
santly, making me wonder, Would this be my own destiny? Is it possible that we Partisans are fated to always
be alone, remain like phantoms...too few in number? I
wondered if the tension and March cold had maddened
me. Just then a rat, nibbling on something, brushed up
against my feet. I shuddered but could do nothing. Somewhere a bell rang, signaling that it was two-fifteen, five-
and-a-half hours since I had become trapped in this
maze of garbage. I wished that by some miracle I could
be allowed to sleep and wake up somewhere else in the
morning.

My feet, my back...my whole body was in terrible pain.
The street had nearly quieted and with great effort I
stood up to urinate, waited a long minute, brushed myself
off and in a half-daze walked away, wondering if at any
second I would be shot. Now that I have lived long enough
to talk freely about it, we had only been able to exist, to
fight and win because the people had shown that they
supported our cause. It was they that hid us and fed us,
and whenever necessary, informed for us.

The same Partisan's formalized statement arrived a month
later:

April 25, 1945. The day finally came, the one we had

long been waiting for. The day for which we, with all the people, had hoped and prepared. The entire city (Milan) was running, shouting and rising up against whoever they considered to be their enemies.

People raced through the streets and alleys embracing each other, embracing us, as they emotionally shouted, 'Long live the *Partigiani!*' It was thrilling to watch as my comrades, the Italian liberation squads, came down from out of the mountains en masse to join in as we rushed from one quarter to another, eliminating the enemy's last strongholds of resistance.

Frightened Fascist officials were being arrested, humiliated, removed beaten and battered by the crowd from offices and basements of their former government buildings. At the same time, German troops that had begun to see the handwriting on the wall had begun surrendering en masse. Was it only hours ago that our Partisan army seemed so few? Now, thank God, we had become a force to be reckoned with. Powerful! And so many!

It had become obvious to the entire populace by then that the Partisans had grown into a considerable force. From the first obscure few, they had now become unmasked as an impressive army of more than 200,000 strong.

Since Mussolini's former importance had been diminished, his Fascist consorts were now inclined to shed their identifying garb and cavalier boots, rather than face the wrath that streamed from Italy's long-suffering citizens.

With the aid of integrated Partisans, many factory workers in larger northern cities like Turin and Milan continued to be indoctrinated on how and when to go on strike.

Manufacturing supplies for the benefit of the Fascists and Germans had intentionally slowed or totally halted. Production of vehicle parts, grain mills, uniforms, anything that required craftsmanship skills that might be helpful to the country's enemies were either on strike or shut down.

All public transportation had been purposely hampered, particularly the flow of goods that in any way might assist Germany's last minute defense.

When a number of Fascist leaning business owners attempted to intimidate their workforce during work stoppages they were greeted with signs and shouts of "Death to Fascism! Out with the Germans! Enough of war!" These were followed by repeated shouts of "Long live the *Partigiani*!" There remained little doubt that the Partisans had physically and psychologically ripped a healthy chunk out of Hitler's war machine.

Everyone dared sense the end was at hand. Widespread insurrection was in the air. The avenues of the big cities now teemed again with a people no longer fearful. But revealing their deep seated fear, German militia still roamed thoroughfares, although in smaller, well-armed groups, and often in buttoned-up armored vehicles. Their cowering Fascist allies that had suddenly resigned their administrative posts began wearing civilian clothes again.

In those last few days before the Allies broke through and into the Valley, the Fascists were sufficiently warned to surrender to authorities of the new Italian government in Rome. Most did rather than face pitiless mobs. For Mussolini's old die-hard crowd there remained little chance of escape.

This unidentified Partisan exemplifies the look and demeanor of many of the 200,000 heroes fighting in the Italian Campaign.

CHAPTER EIGHT

American OSS and the Partisans

Location: Southern Italy, including Anzio and Cassino, then northward along the backbone of Italy's mountain ranges that lead towards Switzerland, France and Austria.

The Situation: German stormtroopers and their Fascist allies were hastily back-pedaling to Italy's colder regions where large hordes of Partisan fighters were intent on retaliating for years of subjugation. Northern Tuscany and Amilia Romagna had become the current killing fields as the war pressed into the frigid Alpine regions that separate Italy from France, Switzerland and Austria.

After their strenuous yearlong drive from Sicily, Allied divisions in Italy suffered from a lack of supplies and reinforcements due to the fact that everything needed for Normandy's D-Day invasion had been relocated to the Britain—understandably a major priority.

Winston Churchill had correctly noted, "General Clark's magnificent army in Italy had to be reduced to a point where it was just enough to produce decisive results against the immense power of the German defensive."

Having already spent the past year uprooting Hitler's army

Goat trails through rugged mountainous areas where the American OSS and
Italian Partisans fought as a team.

out of its defense lines and dugouts below Emilia Romagna, the
gutsy Allies continued to forge ahead with what they had left.
An effort that is still remembered by our troops as being the
most demanding of the entire Italian Campaign. By that time,
the enemy's slave labor forces had more than enough time to set
barbed wire, dig deep tank traps and position gun emplacements
along the rugged peaks that traversed Italy's boot like a wide
garter. Facing the spectre of Germany's preparation in the rugged
terrain, it had become necessary for General Eisenhower to return
a bare minimum of fresh replacements to Italy in order to bolster
crucial points along critical mountain passes and roads. Those
green infantrymen were not as yet battle tested, and the situation
portended an already bloated list of casualties for our weakened
forces that, in the end, became true.

American OSS and Italian Partisans slowly make their way through the steep and narrow mountain trails.

By spring of 1944, American Fifth Army commanders found themselves grasping for any assistance available, especially that which appeared in the form of the recent provincial Partisan groups, which had already been operating within and behind close range of the German front. Though still limited in personnel at that time, the Partisans began to take a noticeable toll on enemy forces. American commanders had begun to perceive that they could be an extremely valuable resource once they were properly led and equipped.

This was a job the American Office of Strategic Service (OSS) had been training to do, and at best, a project that would be extremely difficult to carry out.

The time was ripe for the extraordinary men of the American OSS to participate in the training and assistance of Partisan groups. All those brave Italians needed was a more synchronized approach to their unusual methods, and a fresh, working knowledge of critically needed, up-to-date arms and ammunition. To this end, a profoundly ambitious plan was enacted.

The narratives that occur in this chapter are based on terse, anecdotal reports supplied by both the Partisans and the OSS, along with a synopsis of how the latter came into being. What follows would be less meaningful without the characterization of how those heroic Americans would be chosen.

Before being awakened by Japan's attack on Pearl Harbor, America had been only half-heartedly interested in the affairs of Italy and the puny amounts of information that were received. Those reports had little or no affect on America's politicos whose schedules led them to set aside Mussolini's rape of Africa. Hitler's bristling army had only started to become a worry as his troops munched away at Europe's peaceful states. Britain appeared to be next!

That lax attitude was changed with the alliance formed between Mussolini and Hitler. America could no longer ignore the threat of their warmongering and blustering swagger.

With only a skeleton of secret agents thinly spread throughout the world, sufficient time and strong direction would be required to recruit and train the manpower needed to wage the sorely needed clandestine war. Clearly, American President Franklin D. Roosevelt needed to appoint an extremely imaginative leader for what would become America's first secret militaristic intelligence organization, the OSS.

Roosevelt selected the most obvious choice, General William J. Donovan, to head the new organization. Donovan was known for having an ability to organize and train hastily mobilized regiments during the first World War, and as a major field officer, he would stretch his rigid methods of training almost beyond the breaking point. That facility would be of extreme importance in the building of America's "supermen spies" and the formation of the new agency.

In June 1942, General Donovan immediately set to work developing a plan for what he thought would be needed. Along with the obvious requirements for physical and psychological grooming, the intricate plan would include all manner of training for covert operations, counter intelligence and an extensive knowledge of secret and traditional weapons use.

Dynamic by nature, Donovan had an idea. The United States had a vast number of first generation Americans that were of European parentage. This was especially true of Italian-Americans whose parents were part of a recent wave of immigration. Why not form intelligence units from those first-generation Americans? Their family background and knowledge of the language would certainly make them invaluable warriors, especially behind enemy lines.

On December 23, 1942, Donovan submitted his plan and it was quickly authorized by a Joint Chiefs of Staff directive. It was decided that operatives should be those who learned their foreign language in the home, not in high school or college, and that they should be able to speak the language like the "natives." They would need to know not only the spoken tongue, but also its accompanying facial expressions and bodily gestures, all part of the necessary communication.

After a lengthy period of training, every inductee was to be skilled in the methods of sabotage. Parachutists would be used in groups to operate behind enemy lines and harass the enemy.

Recruiting of the men began in April 1943, and those selected were generally transferred from the army's infantry and engineer companies.

Radio operators were recruited from the Signal Corps, medical technicians from the Medical Corps. All were selected for superior physical qualifications and linguistic abilities.

In actual field experience, their committed units would be divided into OSS Operational Groups (O.G.s) consisting of about sixteen to eighteen men, including at least one field officer. Food, supplies and equipment would be requisitioned from the regular U.S. military, but in the area of other personal services, OSS operatives would have to be self-sufficient and physically adept.

Courses were designed to make all operatives proficient in demolition, small arms (both American and foreign makes), scouting, patrolling and reconnaissance. First aid and unit security measures were also taught, including living off the land, hand to hand combat, fighting with only a knife, camouflage, map reading and compass use, equipment and methods derived and used for airborne and sea-borne raids and willingness to close with the enemy. A liberal education in psychology was given to properly interrogate any enemy they might capture.

Italian Partisans were known to be of varying backgrounds, some being Communist Party advocates, others devoutly religious devotees. In that, OSS personnel were to carefully disregard any and all cultural affiliations

Thus, the OSS had given rise to an aggregate of daring and resolute Americans who indirectly assisted our fighting men, and more often than not, in insular ways.

****

The *Gli Americani e La Guerra di Liberazione in Italia* (Americans and the War of Liberation in Italy), a joint convention held in Venice, Italy, in October 1994, served to commemorate the 50th anniversary of Partisan and OSS interaction during the war. Written and underplayed by those that reported, their wealth of electrifying chronicles provided much to read between the lines, usually unprecedented exploits carried out in joint guerrilla operations. In-depth reports of their combined activities were provided in this rare get together of aged, battle-scarred heroes when Professor Dino Moro, provincial president of the National Association of Italian Partisans of Venice, opened the meeting. He emphasized that its potential dynamic was not intended as a conference of historians but to retell and share personal stories. Narratives were not necessarily presented chronologically, or by any precise geographical construct since the actions had occurred randomly in almost every area of Italy, but mainly in the northern mountains. To extrapolate from those numerous reports would have been a formidable task, leading to this beginning at the epic Anzio adventures.

Allied armies in Italy had been bogged down thirty miles south of Rome along the German Gustav Line where their attack had faltered before the notorious abbey atop Monte Cassino. Overlooking the unobstructed terrain on three sides, Its mountaintop position had become even more insurmountable as a result of the cloister's shattered concrete walls that had once been part of its protective enclosure.

A jagged and dense hurdle, the distorted barricade had become an unintentional gift to the Germans, provided by Allied artillery and numerous air strikes that presented the enemy within a greater protection against repeated attacks. From that advantageous position, their sharp observers could direct salvos of mortar fire even as their infantry warded off attacks from behind the stony rampart. Any attempts to approach the impregnable abbey from east, west or south was suicidal, resulting in a parade of casualties the Allies could ill afford.

The northward drive of our ground troops had come to a dead stop and could only mark time. In order to break out of that strongly held area, Allied leaders Churchill and Eisenhower considered the possibility of a diversionary landing assault somewhere along Italy's enemy controlled coast. The most strategic location appeared to be Anzio, a quiet beach and fishing village less than forty miles south of Rome. If successful, the Allies could easily seize the Alban Hills thirty miles inland, move northward and cut off the German Field Marshall's communication with his 10th Army. It would also force the enemy to retreat to the north or suffer the risk of being caught between two fires, thus leaving the road open to Rome, a prize not to be taken lightly. The outcome could very well affect the balance of the war in Italy.

Untold in the eminent history of Anzio were the crucial roles undertaken by the Partisans. More than was known, their clandestine activities helped prevent a major disaster for the Allies, and ultimately helped turn the tide of battle against the Germans.

For the landing to succeed, it would be necessary to break out of the beachhead as quickly as possible. Allied commanders would need to know how, and in what way, the enemy was likely to respond, making it imperative that the best intelligence available on the mainland had to be at their disposal. Since sea-borne commanders had little, if any, connectivity to the area, it appeared that civilian Resistance groups could be the most helpful. Although their initial offer to assist the Allies by offering to guide their troops through the knotty Alban Hills had been rejected, it was likely that they could provide useful information. It would be useful to discern the strength and location of any German forces in the vicinity, and once operational, the same Partisan agents could also devise crippling diversions that could stall a German retreat. To manage that demanding intelligence task, a highly capable American OSS agent and leader would have to be chosen to organize the area's covert Partisan groups. Such a man would have to be smuggled into Rome prior to the landings, where he would coordinate with the British SOE (Special Operations Executive) that had already been deciphering coded German radio signals. SOE's efforts were beneficial, but much more would be required.

OSS Commander Donovan and 5th Army General Mark Clark immediately agreed on the qualifications of volunteer Peter Tompkins, who spoke Italian like a native. What's more, he had been a war correspondent in Rome prior to working with the OSS, and had already been engaged in several operations with small groups of Roman Partisans. In the process, he had gained their confidence by recruiting and training unaffiliated elements of anti-fascist bands, adjusting their methods of infiltrating and teaching them to spy. All in all, the man was perfect for the project.

Two days before the Anzio landings, Tompkins flew to the island of Corsica ahead of the invasion fleet. During a brisk, moonless night, he set out toward Italy's mainland in a repatriated Italian Navy torpedo boat and arrived at a location one hundred miles north of Rome. He put ashore in a rubber dingy and made his way into the city, revealing afterward that he had encountered several scary moments. One such instant occurred "when a damned Fascist official checked my forged papers near a deserted beach where I had made landfall. It was not without a little trouble and my self-made identity documents. No false documentation services were available to me during those early days."

Having arrived in Rome a day before the Anzio invasion, he was put in touch with a young anti-fascist police officer, Maurizio Giglio, who had been waiting to see him. Somehow, Maurizio had cleverly worked his way through the fighting lines and had brought a radio transmitter from Naples that Tompkins code named "Vittoria." Those radio communications would become extremely valuable to the Allies since Vittoria constantly conveyed significant military intelligence to the beachhead until its transmitting personnel were captured by Nazi SS counterintelligence agents shortly after the breakout.

By then, the damage to the enemy had been done, and Maurizio Giglio had proven to be an extremely exceptional and devoted aide. Unfortunately, he would be betrayed by a double-agent and was cold-bloodedly tortured and executed by the Fascists.

Tompkins asserted in his notes, "Had he chosen to betray me, he could easily have saved himself. Instead he went to his death without saying a word."

For his brave actions, the heroic Partisan's family would receive his posthumous military award, one of the highest reserved for special honors.

Through him, Tompkins had met with another eminent military leader, Partisan Franco Malfatti, who in later years became Italy's Permanent Undersecretary of State for Foreign Affairs. Soon after their meeting, Malfatti readily agreed to deploy almost five hundred Partisans to assist the OSS officer in fulfilling his important mission.

"I had men and women watching every road in and out of the capital, twenty-four hours a day, a complex but rewarding job as all roads lead to Rome," Tompkins recalled later.

Malfatti, who was of Austrian origin, had a concealed source directly involved in German Field Marshall Kesselring's headquarters. That incalculable good fortune allowed Tompkins to become privy to the enemy's daily situation maps on numreous occasions and more.

Another Partisan with whom Tompkins worked was Giuliano Vassalli, wiser by far than his twenty-four years, who also happened to be an Italian Minister of Justice.

In a daring raid, Vassalli and his men released his Partisan comrades, Saragat and Pertini, from prison. Oddly, both of these men were destined to become future Italian Presidents.

As the Socialist representative for the Military Junta of the Roman Committee of National Liberation, Vassalli introduced Tompkins to other heads of the Roman Resistance with whom he would organize activities that would coincide with the final days of the breakout at Anzio.

Tompkins had begun to feel that his fortune was becoming too good to be true, but his and the free world's lucky streak continued, and would benefit the fighting men on the beachhead.

Approximately five minutes before midnight on January 21, 1944, two hundred and fifty ships of the Allied armada silently dropped anchor six miles to the north of the sleepy fishing village of Anzio. At the landing, the Allied forces consisted of 5 cruisers, 24 destroyers, 62 "other" ships, 238 amphibious craft, 5,000 vehicles and 400,000 soldiers. A surrounding darkness enshrouded the already blackened faces of 110,000 American and British infantrymen and sailors who were standing by for a signal. During the ten minutes they waited, salvos of rocket-launchers from the ships opened fire towards suspected German positions near the shoreline. When the thunderous roar of several thousand rounds subsided only an eerie silence echoed back from the beach. Edgy assault teams of amphibious "Operation Shingle" scrambled down the flotilla's mesh ladders into assigned landing craft, not knowing what was in store. For the moment, everything seemed to be in their favor as the sea turned calm and manageable.

The nervous assailants waded ashore, rifles high and waist deep, ready for action, yet the beach remained uncommonly quiet. Their invasion had been uncontested! Later, British General John P. Lucas, in command of the VI Corps, would write, "We achieved what is certainly one of the most complete surprises in history. I could not believe my eyes when I stood on the bridge and saw no opposing fire from the beach."

As dawn approached, the calm plain of the Latium countryside beckoned, stretching inland toward the Alban Hills, and in the unaccountable stillness it appeared that the Allied strategy was about to pay off.

Kesselring's entire German 10th Army had been caught off

guard and outflanked, seemingly destined for obliteration!

Tompkins' narrative continues: "At 10:00 a.m., the morning of the landings, I sat disguised as a military policeman astride a motorcycle alongside Mussolini's former offices in Rome's Piazza Venezia, watching truckloads of heavily armored German paratroopers in their black-and-tan camouflaged uniforms speeding south towards the beachhead. From a building on Corso Umberto, the city's main thoroughfare, I dispatched one of my first Vittoria messages by radio. I could see Germans in the Hotel Plaza hurriedly packing to leave."

That same January morning, the German Field Marshal was heard to say, "Only a miracle could save us."

He was provided that miracle when British General John P. Lucas, in charge of Operation Shingle, commenced what, to this day, remains one of the most controversial actions of the war. Waiting for additional supplies and reinforcements to arrive from England, rather than pursue the element of surprise with haste, turned out to be both an illogical decision and a costly tactical error.

Most histories of the Italian Campaign would reason that the general was incompetent. With the liberation of Rome postponed the situation grew ever more urgent, compelling Allied headquarters to push Tompkins for constantly updated information— trustworthy information that would change minute by minute with every German countermove.

Messages transmitted by Tompkins through Radio Vittoria during the entire beachhead operation were urgent and meant for immediate action. They had begun to be transmitted twenty-four hours a day and well into the final days of the Anzio conflict that continued until early May of 1944—almost five foolishly squandered months. Those transmissions would be remembered in OSS annals as the largest and most dangerous volume of cryptic intelligence ever sent by secret wartime radio. From personalized entries into his autobiographical records, one can see the detailed manner in which he pursued his observations:

> From Kesselring's own situation maps we began to inform the Allied Command of just when and where the Germans were moving, massing or planning to counterattack, and in what force and where they were hiding vital stocks of gas, ammunition or supplies.
>
> The morning of January 24 my inside Partisan sources brought me information indicating where all available German troops within a radius of sixty miles of Rome had been ordered south and moving through Rome the night of the 22nd and 23rd. Among them were three battalions of paratroopers and units of the 90th Panzer Grenadier Division, plus five divisional artillery groups. Units of the 29th and 3rd Panzer Grenadier Divisions were reported transferred from the Garigliano front, moving towards the beachhead. Units of the Hermann Goering Division were moving towards Albano. Another two motorized divisions were reported transferred from Tuscany to the beachhead, one of which was already on its way.

It was estimated that if the Allies launched any kind of attack at the beach, even up to two or three days later, Kesselring would still not have had enough forces in the area to oppose them. Any continued push by the Allies would have affected the roads to the strategic Alban Hills that remained open, and beyond them Rome. Every German general in southern Italy agreed that their troops would have had to be withdrawn, yet the days went by with no Allied follow up materializing. Still puzzled, by the evening of the

24th, the Germans considered that they just might overcome their crisis and had begun to formulate their counterattack.

If the Allies failed to interdict enemy railway traffic at key nodal points, any countermove the Germans attempted would easily provide them enough time to build up their forces faster than the Allies could react.

Warning messages from Tompkins continued and Franco Malfatti's inside sources were always timely and exact. His cryptically scribed information would be rushed to Allied headquarters, as in the following message recorded on January 28th:

UNITS...TWO ARMORED DIVISIONS THROUGH BRENNER TWENTY THIRD TO FIFTH, BOLOGNA VERONA LARGEST CENTERS. BOMB RAILWAY BRIDGE ON PO RIVER. TERNI CIVITA CASTELLANA VERY BUSY. TWO DIVISIONS ALONG COAST SPEZIA CIVITAVECCHIA. FEW DEFENSES OSTIA FREGENE AREA. GROSSETO AND CASTIGLIONE TRASIMENO AIRPORTS ACTIVE. AIRBORNE UNITS ARRIVED GUIDONIA NIGHT TWENTY SIXTH. GERMANS PLANNING LAUNCH HEAVY ATTACK AGAINST BEACHHEAD FOUR HUNDRED HOURS OF SEVENTH.

A constant barrage of similarly fragmented messages had been transmitted to Anzio and Caserta headquarters, often arriving in time to counter and repel a number of the enemy's potential counterattacks.

Allied Command had noted:

Our intelligence got wind through its sources in Rome that the night of the 7th was zero hour and there was a hurried "stand-to" along the Allied lines. The battle that was to lead to the crisis on the beachhead had begun, but the Germans, obviously surprised at unexpected Allied resistance against their planned routes of attack, were again frustrated and unable to push through the heavily protected Allied defenses.

Another section of Tompkins' report to the Venice reunion reads, "All of this intelligence was, of course, gathered by Italian Partisans at great risk and considerable sacrifice: twenty-two of our men were apprehended. They were tortured and butchered in the massacre at Rome's Ardeatine Caves, along with the killing of Maurizio Giglio."

Among General Donovan's historic documents collected and housed in Carlisle, Pennsylvania, is a one-page, undated copy of a letter addressed to President Roosevelt, as well as an identical message to the Joint Chiefs of Staff, in which the General wrote, "An OSS unit hidden in Rome has set up a twenty-four hour watching service on the twenty-one main highways in and out of the capital."

At least five times daily, Tompkins radioed vital intelligence that had been procured by his Partisan agents and the covert operative employed in Field Marshall Kesselrings's headquarters. Among those deserving special praise was an important liaison officer who acted as a spy between the Gestapo in Rome and Mussolini's secret police.

At critical moments during the Anzio action, members of the Roman Partisan team continued to flash word of imminent German counterattacks along the Anzio-Albano axis.

These attacks were repulsed only because G-2 Intelligence at the beachhead had been constantly apprised of where and when they were due from the flow of information supplied by Partisan groups.

Tompkins modestly concluded in his notes, "It is, in any case, the opinion of those against whom these efforts were directed, that it was intelligence, or lack of it, which in the final analysis proved decisive in the battle for Anzio."

When all was said and done, Colonel Langevin, G-2 Intelligence officer of the VI Corps stated, "The OSS might well be said to have saved the beachhead, and to what extent the accumulation of Partisan performance contributed to secure the safekeeping of the Allied beachhead legions remains for historians to decide."

The many important contributions Peter Tompkins made for the eventual triumph at Anzio didn't stop there. He continued to organize Partisan groups that would cope with the enemy in other contentious zones, and as always, behind the lines. His detailed autobiography, *A Spy in Rome*, was published by Simon and Schuster in 1962 and is available from a variety of sources.

I recommend that readers seek out the detailed histories of Anzio's many battle actions. They would have been uncalled for in this publication, but readily found at libraries, bookstores and on the Internet.

****

The Ginny Mission

The OSS had commenced several of their first demanding operations on the French and Italian islands in the Mediterranean Sea. They had been directed from three sources, Allied headquarters in Algeria, the port city of Brindisi on Italy's east coast and Caserta to the west. American and Free French forces had combined with Italian Partisans throughout the area, and in time, these port cities would become main bases for OSS operations.

The prime mission of the OSS was to train and weld a powerful force out of the Resistance fighters, a task that would be arduous

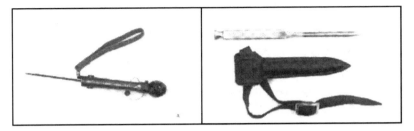

Partisan and OSS clandestine weapons of choice. *Left:* The McGlaglen "Peskett" close-combat weapon; a multi-purpose device containing a knife blade, garrotte and heavily-weighted ball. *Right:* Dagger that could be hidden inside one's sleeve.

but compelling for both the Partisans and O.G.s. A descriptive report by American agent Anthony Scariano sets forth a review of their unbreakable covenant of close and mutual cooperation that existed from September1943 to this very day. Although OSS agents hadn't always alluded to the Partisans in their reports, it should be assumed that wherever O.G.s operated, they required the assistance and collaboration of localized Partisan groups, as in Scariano's anecdotal report that follows:

> On September 17, 1943, the entire 4th group of our O.G. left camp in North Africa and boarded an Italian destroyer sailing for Ajaccio, on the island of Corsica. We were to take part in the Allied invasion of that island.
>
> When our seagoing party landed on the docks that night, we were met by an enthusiastic crowd of French and Italian civilians. (The usual methods of sea transport were by PT boats, Italian Navy submarines or parachute.) They had been waiting for us all day, and as we arrived they shot pistols and rifles in the air, singing the Marseillaise, yelling and dancing with joy. Many

were lighting matches and brandishing flashlights. Houses were lit up and there was no attempt at a blackout or any other form of anti-aircraft security. It was obvious that the Germans had been in the process of retreating northward and only recently had left Ajaccio.

After our arrival, we borrowed several Italian trucks with drivers. The drivers were so pleased to be with Americans and with the rations they received, that they did not want to go back to their own [Partisan] units. Since no one seemed to concern himself with this matter, we kept them around for quite a long time.

We were a small group of fifteen men and had been assigned a definite territory in which to operate. Our mission was to harass the Germans, particularly their vehicular traffic. Each time we encountered small groups of the enemy [evidently rear guard elements], they retreated. In one encounter, however, as we were moving toward the town of Barchetta, on the way to Bastia, we were subjected to heavy and constant mortar fire that killed one of our officers and two of our men. The young lieutenant who was killed had stood out in the road by himself with two hand grenades, and when German vehicles started to come through, he destroyed two of them; one of them an armored car, and the other a truck loaded with troops.

A French Moroccan captain who witnessed this valorous deed stated that it was one of the bravest acts he had ever seen. That area came under constant enemy mortar fire for four days, and the bodies of our dead were not recovered until it ended.

Besides harassing the Germans, we had great success with our mine detectors and removed many mines, and the campaign in which we participated resulted in the expulsion of all German forces from the island of Corsica [an obvious simplification].

After the Corsican campaign was over, we quickly set about to take over the islands of Capraia and Gorgona. [Tiny islands near the kneecap of the boot-shaped Italian peninsula, above Leghorn, to where the group traveled by armed torpedo motorboats.]

After we took those islands, we stationed small complements of enlisted men and one officer on each island, using the islands principally as observation posts against enemy shipping and air activity. We also gathered weather information and verified ship sightings to pass on to our air force units stationed on the island of Corsica. We also furnished information, such as actions in and around Leghorn's gasoline storage base [nearby] to the air force with the result that these bases could be successfully attacked. On more than one occasion, crews of our aircraft were forced to ditch near the islands and were rescued by small Partisan forces there.

We had been aided in the taking of Capraia and Gorgona by Italian torpedo boats and their crews, and many a mission that we conducted from Corsica was carried out with the aid of these splendid craft and their brave young crews. Men with whom we shared not only a close working relationship, but also a deep professional respect and a warm comradery.

When Ginny landed on both islands, we were again surrounded by crowds of happy civilians who gave us enthusiastic receptions. The excitement was electric. Our presence on these two islands also enabled us to warn of any enemy mine-laying operations. Consequently, we were raided several times on both islands. Because we were always less than a dozen men on each island, we had to take to the abundant maquis [evergreen shrubs] without delay because the Germans always outnumbered us on these forays by at least thirty or forty to one. Of course, they'd be very quick hit-and-run raids carried out at night because the enemy could not afford to be exposed on the sea in daylight. They would usually try to wreck our radio installations and take a number of civilian prisoners in order to obtain whatever information they could from them as to our activities.

Ginny's operations from Corsica continued mainly to cause enemy alerts along the Italian coast from south of Leghorn to the Rome seaport of Civitavecchia, carrying out harassing raids and other missions that would cause the Germans to believe that we were reconnoitering for possible invasion points. That caused the enemy to deploy their forces accordingly. Corsica would occasionally be swept by strafing fire from German fighter planes, and Bastia would be shelled by German destroyers. On one occasion, the Germans succeeded in mining the approaches to the harbor in Bastia, which resulted in blowing up an LST and its escorts.

We also conducted nocturnal hit-and-run operations such as putting small teams ashore on the Italian coast to blow up bridges and other targets, cutting the enemy's lines of communications, ascertaining enemy dispositions, etc. In one of our raids on the island of Pianosa [near Capraia], which we conducted with French assistance, we killed several Germans and took twenty-four prisoners. Our only casualty was one Frenchman wounded.

On the night of 20/21 February 1944, the Germans raided Capraia with several landing craft and an escort of E-boats. I was sent with help and supplies from Bastia with a PT boat to investigate as soon as we had word from our complement on Capraia that the island had been raided, and we very carefully mine spotted the shallow waters while going in and coming out of the island's tiny port. On my return to Bastia, I made my report to my commanding officer as to the damage done on Capraia, which was slight, and I reported also that the enemy appeared to have achieved very little for the size of the raiding party they had used.

The planning and execution of our operations from Corsica were many and varied, but the one that will remain most vivid in our memory was one that we attempted to carry to a successful conclusion on the night of 22/23, March 1944. A team of thirteen enlisted men and two officers in U.S. Army uniforms were given the assignment of blowing up the entrances to two railroad tunnels on the La Spezia-Genoa rail line, roughly 500 yards southeast of Stazione Framura [a railroad station between Pisa and Genoa].

American O.G. Major Materazzi, who was then a first lieutenant, commanded the operation, which was attempted to be carried out with the use of two American PT boats.

I say "attempted" because we were not successful in fully executing the plan. This operation is one of many which impel us most strongly to return to Italy to share with you our triumphs and our sorrows as participants in the Italian Resistance Movement, the story of which we hope will be fully recorded and appreciated on both sides of the ocean through the medium of what we have been doing here in Venice [the meeting] and throughout northern Italy.

Landfall was made west of Stazione Framura, where the PT boats disembarked members of the team into rubber dinghies on the night of March 22nd. When the small rubber boats reached shore, about fifteen to twenty minutes later, the shore party made contact with the command PT offshore informing us that they thought they had found the target

However, about five minutes later an enemy convoy was sighted by one of the PT boats, which alerted the other PT, and passed as a convoy to the west of one of the PT boats. The convoy fired all of its guns to seaward as if it were being attacked or as if it thought that it was being attacked. During the next three hours, a succession of enemy craft appeared in the area, and the PTs successfully evaded them. As soon as a rendezvous between the two PT boats was affected, the steering gear of one of them failed. By this time, it was apparent that the enemy was searching the area by plane and ships.

At approximately four in the morning, the decision was made by the naval officers and the OSS officers to return to Bastia without recovering the party from the beach because eight enemy ships were in the immediate vicinity of the point at which the landing party was to be picked up after the operation had been completed. One of our PTs was mechanically helpless; and the time that it would take to reach the beach and pick up the party and return to the assistance of the crippled PT boat would have placed the boats within sight of the beach in daylight and subject to probable attacks from the air and from German shore batteries. A major element of concern was the security of the radar from being captured. Because the enemy had nothing like it, great care would have had to be taken to avoid having that valuable equipment fall into their hands. Arrangements had been made in advance as part of the plan of operations to pick up the landing party the following night in the event we could not have accomplished it that same night. Contact was lost with the shore party about twenty minutes after the landing party arrived, and it was not re-established that night.

Attempts to pick up the team again were made the following night but it ran into heavy enemy patrols offshore. All attempts to get within walkie-talkie range with anyone on the beach were unsuccessful because of the large number of patrol craft guarding the area, so the rescue party retired.

Another attempt was made the following night but the weather was too bad.

Therefore, a final attempt was made on the night of 25/26 March to recover the party, again without success. On the 25th, both the German and [Fascist] Italian radios broadcast a communiqué that an American commando raiding party had been annihilated near La Spezia. Nothing was heard for many months. In April of the following year, when the American 5th Army had advanced far enough along the Italian coast, we learned from residents in the area that after some fighting, all of our men were captured without serious injury. They were taken to La Spezia, interrogated by the German command, and within forty-eights hours thereafter, were

taken to a lonely point along the coast and executed by
the Germans. We found and identified their bodies, still
clothed in American Army uniforms, their hands bound
with wire behind their backs. The examinations conducted by our doctors showed that the skull of each
man had been crushed and that there were no bullet
holes in the bodies or skulls. In 1990, OSS officers attended a ceremony sponsored by the University of Genoa
and the Ligurian Partisans for the dedication of a museum
and study center. They also arranged to have a marble
plaque in memory of the Ginny victims placed in the Piazza at Ameglia, the town near which the OSS team was
murdered. Their bodies now lie in a U.S. cemetery.

****

During the time of Scariano's adventures along Italy's west
coast, the British secret service, in a joint operation with the
OSS, carried out the Simool Mission on the eastern coast. This,
with the realization that the mission would operate with similar
instructions to find prisoners of war who might have been liberated after the 1943 Italian truce with the Allies. Our intelligence
had requested additional information regarding the enemy's
strength along the opposite strip of coastline.

In late September, the Simool Mission led the O.G. to rendezvous with British agents at various points from Pescara to
Ancona along the eastern Adriatic Sea.

Lieutenant Peter Sauro headed one of Simool's O.G.s that had
secretly infiltrated by air and sea into an area suspected of har-
boring a force of German commandos. A number of men, including Lt. Sauro, were captured. A few managed to escape but
Sauro was not successful. He and the others were forced to
remain prisoners of war in Germany and lived to tell of his har-

rowing saga after being released at the conclusion of the Italian Campaign in 1945.

By the time the remainder of Simool's agents completed their mission in 1945, a conservative computation by Allied Command estimated that over 2,000 Allied prisoners had been rescued by their actions. In joint assignments with Partisan auxiliaries, American O.G.s would have amassed a voluminous list of rescue missions. Along with those already noted, the extensive list of oddly titled mission names would include the following, which illustrates only a portion of those that existed:

These, and other Partisan/OSS missions would be so damaging to the enemy that they prompted this intercepted telegram, dated 26 February 1945, from German Field Marshall Kesselring to his supreme commander in Berlin:

MISSION TITLE	AREAS OF ACTION
Bathtub II	Sardinia
0Simool	S.E. Italy
0 OP 2	Capraia
0Polar 1	Italian West Coast
0Polar 2	Italian West Coast
0 OP 3	Italian West Coast
Neptune	Leghorn (Livorno)
Valentine	Genoa
Chicago 1	Pianosa
Alpha	Anzio
Chicago 2	Pianosa
Ginny 1	Mediterranean islands
Balkis 1	Pianosa
Balkis 2	Piano
Walla Walla	Liguria
Chrysler	Como and vicinity
Ford	Val D'Aosta
Aztec	Belluno and vicinity

MISSION TITLE	AREAS OF ACTION
Cayuga	Parma
Tacoma	Cortina d'Ampezzo and vicinity
Spokane/Sewanee	Val Tellina
Santee	Sondrio
Roanoke	Piacenza and vicinity
Choctaw	Parma and vicinity

Activity of Partisan bands on the Western Apennines, and along the Via Emilia, particularly in the areas of Modena, Reggio and Parma, and southwest of them, as well as near the neighborhood of Piacenza, has spread like lightning in the last ten days. The concentration of Partisan groups of varying political tendencies into one organization, as ordered by the Allied High Command, is beginning to show clear results. The success of Partisan operations shows considerably more of their commanding leadership.

Up to now it has been possible for us, with a few exceptions, to keep our vital rear lines of communications open by means of our slight protective forces, but this situation threatens to change considerably for the worse in the immediate future. Speedy and radical countermeasures anticipate this development. It is clear to me that our only remedy, and one which is unavoidably necessary to meet the situation, is the concentration of all our available forces, even if this means temporary weakening in other places.

I request of you therefore to combine with 14th Army and the Army of Liguria in carrying out several large scale operations which will nip in the bud the increasing activity of Partisan bands in Northern Italy. Please let

me have your proposals as to when these measures can
be carried out, and with what forces.

(signed) Kesselring

By contrast, a Letter of Commendation addressed to the American Commanding Officer, 2671st Special Reconnaissance Battalion, was received from General Mark W. Clark, Headquarters, Fifth Army Group. The following is a paragraph from his notes:

The task of the men of your company was a difficult one as they were constantly pursued and harried by enemy forces. With the knowledge that if captured, they probably would be tortured and executed by the enemy, these men volunteered for extra hazardous missions. The outstanding success of Partisan operations in the areas where these men operated, and the excellent intelligence as to enemy dispositions received was, in large measure, due to the presence of these men and their leadership of Partisan formations.

Another graphic remembrance was freely translated from an anecdotal statement obtained at the Venice meeting from Partisan hero, Renato Pensa. His area of operation had been located along the Ligurian Alps, in Italy's northwest. Towns and rivers mentioned are located between Monte Carlo, France, and Turin, Italy.

Pensa and his group were reinforced with the British 8th Army's 1st Alpine Division complement that included Maori, special New Zealand troops who were joined with the Partisans in battles that occurred along the westernmost peaks of Italy's Maritime Alps. OSS missions in that area had, on occasion, made contact with Maori commanders who freely offered as much assistance to the OSS as needed.

In the brutal winter of 1944-45, the OSS Morristown Mission had been guided by American O.G. leader Maurizio Fracassi. He had parachuted into a mountainous area near the Piedmont village of Soglio Monferrato. The mission had advised the Partisans that they would be receiving their supplies from across the steep French border, trails that consisted of summit crossings at altitudes of up to 3,000 yards requiring a considerable amount of mountain-climbing experience.

During that period the Partisan fighting force in the Italian/French Alpine zone had grown to a considerable force of about 6,000 men. Not only did they carry out guerilla warfare against German and Fascist troops, but by their very nature, also occupied and defended vast areas that included entire villages.

Major Temple, the head of a British S.O.E. mission in the locale, had pushed for a landing strip to be constructed in Partisan country. Such an airfield would greatly simplify the supply problems that it lacked, and had been the main hindrance for Partisan groups who actively pursued the enemy in that difficult mountainous zone.

It would have also ensured easy and rapid connections with Allied Headquarters in Southern Italy and easier repatriation of the countless Allied soldiers who were recuperating in the hospitals in that zone that had already been liberated.

After having reconnoitered the area, Major Temple, along with several Partisan lieutenants, chose a location along a comparatively large clearing along the right bank of the Bormida River. It wasn't long before the Partisans provided hundreds of men armed with shovels and pickaxes to level the ground, and with a good number of oxen and horses, dragged heavy stonerollers to compact it. Within ten days a narrow 30 x 900 meter runway was ready. The Major named it "Excelsior," probably the first of other crude landing strips to be fabricated by the Partisans behind the front lines.

In November 1944, a four-engined aircraft carried out a daytime supply drop to Partisans that had joined with the O.G. of the 1st Langhe Mission in the area of Cuneo.

Without losing height, the plane dropped its containers by parachutes fitted with barometric capsules connected to small explosive charges, which were designed to make them open near the ground, but at a height which would not cause damage to the inner material. The area was situated in a basin between two mountainous rises and some of the loads had dropped over the high ground, falling among the cliffs. Several newly designed special parachutes partly softened the impact, while all the loads that were launched into the valley did manage to reach the ground intact. Fortunately, the launch was not seen from far off, but could have been very risky, especially for the integrity of the materials waiting within them.

The following day, November 12th, the Partisan 1st Division received a second daytime resupply from fifteen B-24s that carried out their drops in the traditional method, with those loads arriving in perfect order. It was a clear autumn day with visibility extending several miles. This time the area of drop, Marsaglia, clearly displayed hundreds of multicolor parachutes that descended to the ground in a most spectacular way. Regretfully, that flashy drop was also seen by nearby Nazi-Fascist garrisons that in the night attacked the Partisan/O.G. positions along the banks of the river and followed up with a series of scathing, prolonged attacks on all the posts of the 1st Langhe Division. The German 34th Division, combined with Mussolini's Fascist Republican companies, were now drawn up against the Allied mission with a crushing force of six battalions supported by heavy armor.

The fierce fighting on both sides lasted from November 13th to 17th, in an area along the left bank of the Tanaro River that in its wake took the life of Major Temple during the most critical mopping-up stage. In a local hospital where he had been taken, and as badly wounded as he was, he seized at the opportunity to talk with the Maori commander who attempted to cheer him. Even in the calming conversation that followed, Major Temple emphasized the excellent fighting and retreat tactics of the Partisan troops, comparing their work to that of which only a few well-trained armies could have boasted. He then gave other words of encouragement before being transferred to the hospital in Cortemilia, which was considered to be safer and better equipped at that moment, but he died that night. The Allies had lost a brave officer and a great friend.

To ensure the continuing support of the Resistance forces on the ground under such difficult circumstances, the immediate replacement of a sharp-witted Allied officer was necessary to continue Temple's exigent communications.

On November 17th, a Lysander (a British single engine plane) landed at the airstrip to determine and report on the airstrip's functionality.

Two days later, on November 19th, an American B25 "Mitchell" bomber appeared over the strip and landed after accomplishing a difficult maneuver. It had brought a new leader, Lieutenant Colonel Stevens, to replace Major Temple as coordinator for the diverse Allied missions in the area. Without stopping its engines, the B25 took on twenty-five needy passengers and departed for Pisa.

During the next few days, a Mitchell was hit by flak during a low altitude bombing run on the bridges over the Po River. The crew and its cargo escaped capture, thanks to Partisan efforts to protect them. On another Mitchell, six men were hit by anti-aircraft fire, its grounded crew saved after a gunfight with the Germans by Partisans of the 6th Division and the timely appearance of a formation of American fighter planes.

Airstrip operations came to an abrupt halt on November 20, 1944, during the enemy's fierce attack along the Bormida valley. Although they had done their best to resist, the Partisans were forced to retreat into the safety of adjacent areas. One of their brigades had remained close to the contentious zone, and with especially chosen men and an attachment of American O.G.s, they continued their guerrilla actions against the Germans through the entire month of December until January 1945.

In February, a great number of Fascist units had pushed into the Bormida valley. Their mop-up operation lasted about one week, and after another fierce battle, sixteen Partisans of the Savona Partisan Brigade and 102nd Garibaldi Division, lay dead. The besieged Savona group had been led by American Lieutenant Placido Faro. Known by the Partisan title "Bambu," he had been highly respected by the Partisans, but he too was killed and lay alongside his Italian comrades. A posthumous Silver Medal and Purple Heart would be presented to his family.

During their Venice reunion, OSS officer Mario Fiorentini reported on the Texas Mission and the actions of Partisan Alfredo Michelagnoli, who seemed to be intimately known among those in attendance by his nom de guerre as "Fred."

Giaime Pintor, Paolo Petrucci, Augusto de Cobelli and Jacopo Barsotti had been persuaded by Fred to leave their homes and families to join him in the battle for Anzio. They, among others, had followed him deep into the environs of Anzio and worked closely with Peter Tompkins, completing his endeavors closer to the action.

Fred and his cadre of Resistance fighters had hoped to fight side by side with the beleaguered Allied army by enlisting many more Partisans from the neighboring areas around Anzio's coastal plain. During one of his initial forays into unknown territory, their noble purpose proved fatal for Partisan Pintor who was blown to bits by a German land mine on the banks of the Volturno River. Not long afterward, Petrucci felt a need to return to his ailing wife in Rome, where he was arrested and tortured by the Fascist police. Apparently, an acquaintance he trusted had turned informer. Petrucci was executed with others who had been operating in the city and massacred at the Fosse Ardeatine's killing grounds.

After many weeks of contacting Resistance groups in and around the Latium area, Fred succeeded in assimilating an impressive intelligence service. His men were known to have forcefully held and safeguarded a number of Allied bridgeheads between Rome and Anzio.

Among the first OSS Operational Groups in the Italian Campaign, the Texas Mission expertly demonstrated its true value. In one situation its network of Partisans flashed the news of a pending German counterattack that provided Allied commanders near the beach, time to set up a stronger zone of opposition. Many American and British lives had been saved that day from the onslaught that, in all probability, would have occurred.

The following is written in the OSS records regarding the Texas Mission and that singular action:

> The Texas Mission accomplished an excellent service. The information it supplied helped immeasurably to break through the enemy's counterattacks at the Anzio front. It played an important part in directing and coordinating the Resistance Movement in the city of Rome and helped in the actual liberation of the city of Rome.

After Rome had been liberated, OSS General Donovan praised an assemblage of Fred and his men, and finished his speech with a deservedly enthusiastic compliment: "You and your men have done the work of a full division of soldiers!"

After Anzio, Fred's Texas Mission went on to make further significant contributions, and took him to battles in the vicinity of Rome's Latium region, and later the Veneto coastal district. With arms and ammunition obtained through airdrops, Fred and his men took part in bloody encounters at Monterotondo, which resulted in the killing seventy-five German soldiers, scores of enemy wounded, the capture of more than one hundred prisoners and the destruction of three Mark IV tanks.

American President Harry Truman awarded Fred the Bronze Star Medal in February 1944, and listed his actions in a large number of operations the heroic leader had been involved in.

The Venice report suggests that more of Fred's documents should have been made available, but their histories were incomplete. "We know for certain that Michelagnoli [Fred], in the last few years of his life, destroyed more than a few papers referring to his wartime experiences. That was his right. But Fred was a man of few words and rarely confided his own combat experiences to friends. Those experiences had allowed him to meet free, courageous and loyal men."

Nevertheless, Fred's accomplishments would be forever remembered by those who shared the battlefield with him.

****

Largely due to the early successes of American missions, the British Army's huffy attitude towards "those bloody American Yanks" soon eased. Strained relationships were quickly forgotten after their soldiers learned to appreciate the daring actions of the OSS. Having observed those uncalled for parochialisms, Partisan Commander Mario Fiorentini, explained them with sensitive perceptiveness in his notes at the Venice meeting:

Discord between the British and American points of
view had been obvious, and ultimately interpreted by Italians as "differences of opinions of the conservative
Churchill compared to the democratic Roosevelt." It was
well known that the English, in the first stage of the
Italian campaign, aimed to set up their own nuclei of informers, disregarding the newly formed Partisan groups,
but that chauvinism was soon abandoned. It would have
been almost impossible to operate radio-transmitting and
other covert missions without strong American OSS and
Partisan cooperation.

Fortunately, the dogma did not last. It couldn't be ignored that
the Allied Army consisted of a vast range of world-wide inter-
nationals. Their troops had participated in cracking the strongly
defended German Gustav Line and others when Casino was finally penetrated by the Free French colonial forces, followed by
the daring Polish infantry who attacked the abbey at Monte
Cassino. The Pole's seized it with a considerable loss of men
and its capture led to the speedy northward advance towards
Rome by the American 5th and British 8th Army.

The German Army began a hurried retreat and most of its
troops in the Alban Hills had come under the relentless hammering of combined Allied armor and artillery. Rome would shortly
be in Allied hands, but a heady question remained: Would the
famous capitol be spared the devastation that had been the hallmark of the malicious enemy as they pulled out? Fortunately,
the Germans didn't have time to tarry and had taken flight towards
the nearby Tuscan hills, Siena and Florence, leaving Rome an
"open city."

With Germany's retreat to the new battle lines, Fred and his
men returned to the capitol where he had been stealthily gathering
additional Partisan forces. Intensely revitalized with the recent

Allied success, he could not wait for a better time to lead his Partisans toward battles that erupted in Italy's more northern provinces. But it would be another long and bloody year before his vehemence would be completely satisfied.

Fred and Fiorentini found Rome's remaining Partisan groups fragmented, and in sore need of renovating their previous zeal after the long hiatus at Cassino. He was sure that fired up and properly governed, he would have an easier time inciting them to action. Man by man and group by group, they regenerated the Roman Partisans, reviving their motivation and rousing them to proceed northward towards where they were most needed. Having waited so long to put their plans into practice, the two men and their army of rebels were now ready to tackle new projects away from home.

Captain Domenic Rocchi, Mario Gaudiosi and Major Rocchi, all former Italian army officers, had become invaluable colleagues to Commander Fiorentini.

They, along with several empathetic *carabinieri*, became group leaders and were at their commander's side throughout the next action-filled year. Such an assortment of Partisan officials presented much-needed military competence when called upon to handle uncommon battle assignments.

Their well-drilled Partisans were known to defend Tuscany's more pastoral brothers from unremitting German raids on their farms and livestock, and through ingrained kinship developed good will among the rural populace. Their charitable benevolence paid off on many occasions, especially when they received un-expected assistance from amiable farmers who supplied them with important information or shelter.

Late one May night, in the darkness of a refuge in Tivoli, Sal-vatore di Benedetto showed Partisan Commander Fiorentini and Captain Lucia Ottobrini, his second in charge, the details of plans he had prepared for defending a section of power plants north of Rome.

Di Benedetto had just left when one of his companions was caught in a heavy bombing raid that rendered him permanently disabled. Lucia, who had remained in the old stucco refuge, noticed large cracks appearing in the walls and miraculously escaped.

Fiorentini's report regarding Partisan actions on the northern outskirts of Rome served to demonstrate his skill in shaping and unifying personnel. He wrote:

> With the help of Giorgio Formiggini, Valentino Gerratana, Cesare Colombo, Aldo Natoli and others a precious intelligence service was set up.
>
> Reports of German troop movements, enemy placements and depots, and every possible information of use for the war program to be delivered to OSS Regional Headquarters. I had arranged two fields for receiving airdrops to be prepared along the hillside of Monte Gennaro, and another along the high ground dominating the Empolitana Way. The importance of those receiving locations cannot be overstated since men and supplies were gratefully received and used to the best advantage.

Almost a year after Rome was retaken, Fiorentini and a Partisan group had been operating 260 miles beyond Rome. The city was Milan, and the focus of the leader's attention was the town square, Piazzale Loreto, where Mussolini's body would be displayed after being captured and killed.

> On July 18, 1944, we are continuing to push north. I was parachuted into a mountain district among the patriots of the Justice and Liberty Brigade led by Fausto

Cossu. I had received orders to establish a contact with the Volunteer Corps of Liberty Headquarters in Milan through the milliner Brenna, who ran a small milliner's shop in the city. I had been designated to be a liaison officer with the Partisan formations of North Italy, to whom I would transmit the instructions given by the new legitimate Italian Government which had been set up in Rome.

First of all I had to cross the mobile line of the front that separated the zone controlled by Partisans from the German occupied territory.

Enrico Anguissola and his young close relation, Alberto, accompanied me as far as Piacenza, where I met the C.L.N. [Committee of National Liberation] chiefs.

After leaving my two companions to reach Milan, I committed the rash act, never thereafter repeated, of catching a local train. Just the other side of the Po River [forty miles south of Milan], a patrol of Germans stopped the train and made all the younger men get off, taking them to a barracks near Codogno. As prisoners, they immediately set us to excavating and strengthening the ground on either side of the river, where fortifications and anti-aircraft artillery had been set up and well camouflaged by the dense vegetation. We mostly worked at night.

The next day, while working, I took advantage of the confusion caused by an unexpected burst of machinegun fire. It was like repeating the scenario that I experienced when I was digging in the rubble behind the Anzio front in the spring of '44. I escaped and after a long trek through the fields, reached a small house where I found Rosetta and Giuseppe Croce, two veritable Partisans, who,

from then on, were of great help to me in many difficult
and dramatic moments. With their help I finally reached
Milan. Passing through Piazzale Loreto, I saw the shocking sight of the corpses of fifteen Partisans left lying on
a pavement under a petrol pump. They had been shot by
the Fascists after having been transported from Rome's
San Vittore prison. This sustained me during the hard,
dramatic moments of the war in Rome, which upon leaving for the North, I had intended burying.

I presented myself that afternoon with the password
agreed upon by the milliner Brenna, by which I could
get in contact with Francesco [Umberto Massola], Fabio
[Pietro Vergani] and Giorgio Amendola. I told the latter
what I had seen in Piazzale Loreto. I also described to
him the episode of Carlo Salinari, who only by chance
had escaped the massacre. I also reminded him of the
repeated attempts to escape made by other Partisans. In
addition, I made comparisons between the conditions in
which we had been obliged to fight in extremely clandestine circumstances and the situation of the valleys
in Liguria and Lombardy, which I had just visited at a
moment in which the Partisan formations were being
numerically strengthened.

Thousands of youths wishing to enlist were held as
reserves because we did not have enough arms...they
had been responding to the furious mopping-up operations that moved large units from the front. We also
discussed the necessity of taking measures to strengthen
the single HQ of the 13th Zone. Giorgio told me at a
later meeting that it had been decided that I was to leave
the transmitter set and radio operator at the 13th zone
HQ, and that I was to go back and forth between the

Ligure-Emilia Mountain passes [alpine mountain area west of Lake Maggiore].

In my journeys to and from Milan I was to cross the Po by boat, which I often did, sometimes with the help of Rosetta and often with a Partisan comrade who lived near Caselle Landi.

In early Fall 1944, it had been wrongly believed that the Allied troops together with the Italian Fighting Groups would have soon occupied the Po estuary and then stormed into the Padana plain, forcing the Germans to move their defense lines back to the Valtellina and Alto Adige rivers, where the mountain ranges would have provided a satisfactory bulwark. Alfredo Michelagnoli [Fred], Commander of the OSS Texas Mission, had taught me that the radio missions should always try to stay in the enemy-occupied area and avoid being "liberated" by advancing friendly troops.

I was given an example of this by Pertini and Amendola, when they left Rome for Milan too soon, before the capital was liberated. A perilous move for both. For this reason I willingly obeyed the order to move from the western Apennines and go further north to operate in the Milan-Como-Sondrio triangle.

The following three months of Fiorentini's actions were compacted into a report by Giorgio Amendola, an American OSS man, and retold in the following paragraphs.

Mario Fiorentini had organized an intelligence network that branched out into parts of Liguria where he had periodic contacts with the Partisan Ligurian Brigade. Apparently, he had set up supporting bases everywhere. This fearless soldier did not hesitate to infiltrate any important German defense system around the

Po, and by night obtained information that included the posi-
tioning of some sixty anti-aircraft and anti-tank pieces, along
with their exact coordinates.

In a short time he had acquired the extraordinary ability to
pass through the network of fixed and mobile roadblocks that
the German and Fascist Republican Army had closed all around
Partisan controlled areas. He had been arrested several times by
the Fascists and the Germans, but always managed to escape.
How he did remains obscure.

As the appointed head of the Dingo Mission, Fiorentini had
constantly been on the move, parachuting behind the enemy's
Gothic Line along the Apennines and operating out of four adjoining regions in northern Italy—Emilia, Liguria, Lombardy and
Piedmont. For his actions in Anzio, then to the northernmost
boundaries of Italy, he was awarded three silver medals for Military
Valour and three Crosses for Merit from the Italian government,
hardly enough for the hero he most assuredly was.

****

The Tacoma Mission

*Location: Tyrolean Alps in the territory of Venezia-Giulia, in-
cluding the cities of Venice, Cortina d' Ampezzo and Trieste.*

Thoughts and recollections reported by OSS Agent Howard
W. Chappel follow. His extremely dangerous assignments were
presented in Venice, and without a hint of grandiloquence, made
his experiences sound like child's play.

Fifty years ago, I was honored to join with many
brave men and women who participated in the defeat of
the Nazi forces in Northern Italy. The Germans had in-

vaded, pillaged and murdered as they conquered their neighbors in Europe.

Many heroes of many nations ultimately led to the destruction of the Nazi machine and denied them the world conquest they had sought.

Those Americans who lived in safety in the United States could never truly understand the misery and suffering of the gallant people who were overrun by the savage invaders of Hitler's legions. However, American production at home provided the war materials needed to make possible the defeat of the Germans and Japanese. It was the sons and daughters of Americans who joined the military forces and traveled to all parts of the world to engage these enemy savages.

In the beginning, America was poorly equipped for the magnitude and ferocity of the conflict that was thrust upon Europe by the Nazis.

America, like a sleeping giant, awoke and initiated the greatest emergency arms mobilization the world had ever seen. In times of great national peril, a great nation must have great leaders to defend that nation and its causes. If those leaders do not exist, then that nation must fall. Our president was such a great leader, and he delegated other great leaders to implement and direct our mobilization. For the first time in history, the United States embarked on a program of covert operations.

History has proven the value of the OSS to the final outcome of World War Two. I hope that the history of Resistance will include more facts and details concerning General Donovan. A hero of World War 1, he had been awarded the Congressional Medal of Honor.

In October 1943, I was transferred from the Army

Parachute Troops to the OSS in Washington, D.C. to
do duty in Germany. Sent to Oran in Algiers and unable
to make arrangements for a German mission, I and my
men wound up in Siena where the Free French and our
Operational Groups had been functioning. There I felt I
finally had a home.

In November 1944, we were offered a mission with
an Italian group in Northern Italy, with the objective
being the area around the Brenner Pass. It was not ad-
visable to take the whole group at one time, nor were so
many men needed at a time. Accordingly, on December
26, Sgt. Fabrega, Sgt. Silsby and I jumped near Trichiana
[forty-five miles north of Venice] where we temporarily
joined with the Aztec Mission. We were received at the
Partisan 7th Alpini group by Commander Checco. While
we waited for the snows to recede so that we could travel
north, we joined with both Tollot and Mazzini Partisan
brigades. On February 21, I received three more [Amer-
ican] men, Sgt. Delanie, Sgt. Ciccone and Sgt. Buckhardt.
The latter was a medic, the other two were weapons
and demolition experts. From the inception of the mission, Tacoma was in almost constant action against the
German forces, and twice against Fascist troops. Most
of our actions were in cooperation with the Tollot, commanded by Paolo, whom I called "Yankee Doodle," and
the Mazzani, commanded by Bruno. Both men were outstanding leaders.

In April 1945, we moved north to join with the Partisan
Val Cordevole Brigade, commanded by Ettore. I had lost
Fabrega and Silsby, who had been captured on March 6th.

Because of the difficulty of moving too many men at
one time, I left Sgt. Delanie with the Partisan Piave
Brigade. Sgt. Ciccone, Sgt. Buckhardt, a radio operator,

a Partisan named Gigi, and I had been concealed in a truck, then proceeded to Caprile where we met Ettore. In cooperation with him and his men, we continued activity against the Germans until their surrender. The balance of the O.G. who were not in the Tacoma mission served in other areas. Captain Taylor and some of the men served as part of another mission in Italy. Many of the men served as Jump Masters, making drops of personnel and supplies to Partisans and Allied missions. Sgts. Fabrega and Silsby were somehow freed from their Prisoner of War camp, where they had been held near Merano, and returned to us. With the end of the war, we departed Italy with both joy and regrets. We were happy to go home, but sorry to leave so many good friends and Partisan comrades. I have not mentioned all the many people among the Partisan resistance to whom our mission owes a deep regard for in America, but we still had a war in the Pacific against the Japanese to think about.

****

The Mangosteen-Chrysler Mission

Location: North of Milan, in the mountainous area between Lake Maggiore and Lake Orta.

Unforgettable experiences had engraved their mark on the list of heroes that took part in these combined missions. Paladins that fought and fell in the name of peace, social justice and freedom, with no compensation for their enormous sacrifices other than knowing the righteousness of their cause. Partisan Rino Pacchetti's report speaks for itself, his passionate words proffered among analogous others at the assembly.

I want to speak here about the Mangosteen-Chrysler Mission, perhaps the most significant organized in occupied Italy, and to which were entrusted tasks of extremely great importance. The OSS was an information, counter-espionage and strategic operations service in territory behind the lines of combat. It was the 2677 Regiment that operated in Italy, with jurisdiction over all operators within the Mediterranean Basin.

Our group was involved with Secret Intelligence, counter-espionage, operation groups, Special Operations and moral operations. The mission was parachuted onto Mottarone [a mountain that separates Lake Maggiore from Lake Orta] on September 26, 1944, at about 11:30 p.m. At that time, two brigades of my division were operative in that zone, the VALTOCE, then commanded by Alfredo Di Dio [Marco], who subsequently fell in combat during heavy fighting and was awarded the Medal of Honor in memoriam.

The mission was made up of seven components who were all dependent on OSS, even if they each undertook different tasks.

The Chrysler Mission, almost straight away transferred itself to the area of Lake Orta and made immediate contact with what was of the greatest importance—the information activities supplied by Surveyor Aminta Migliari [Giorgio], a legendary figure of a man, both saboteur and fighter.

The destruction of the railway bridge at Pettenasco was his achievement, and much owed to Giorgio for the fact that after the two heavy losses sustained in the conflicts with the Nazi-Fascists and the loss of its heroic leader Alfredo Di Dio [Marco], the "Valtoce" division was able to reorganize itself. Giorgio was a decisive help, giving me vital information, enabling me to identify zones where the missing and injured were gathered and for the recovery of arms and ammunition with a total of 950 men. To facilitate matters, Giorgio put at my disposal a patrol of eighteen Partisans belonging to the San Maurizio d' Opaglio group.

The Chrysler Mission of which Paccheti had spoken, was based on Isola San Giulio, an atoll in Lake Orta. It would be there that they received support from the official Partisan Information Services in the form of two experts, Giuseppe Manini and Gualtiero Tozzin, whose bravery and knowledge made them equal to the hazardous task ahead. With almost perfect precision, they developed a network so extensive as to enable them to monitor all movements of the Nazi-Fascist forces in the northern Italian states of Piedmont and Lombardy, Liguria, the Veneto and Emilia Romagna, a territory the area the size of Austria.

If forced to retreat to their own country, the Germans would have to pass through those five operational zones. Even there, the Partisans were prepared to call on a network of trusted civilian informers, mostly railway workers and clergymen.

In the province of Piedmont, near the busy city of Turin, the work of Professor Maria Giulia Cardini [Ciclone] and Professor Aldo Quartetta handled an exchange of information that was of enormous value to Allied-Partisan groups. Especially when it came to "neutralizing" the railway wagons filled with TNT, which the Germans and Fascists ordered into the high reaches of the Val d'Ossola, near Switzerland, in order to blow up dams and hydro-electric plants. Had they been successful, it would have been a major blow to much of Italy's northern region. Apart from the loss of human lives and consequent ecological disaster, it could have left the provinces of Lombardy and Piedmont without electrical energy for at least six to seven years. Thanks to the intelligence supplied by railway-workers, Pacchetti's men were able to intercept those deadly cargoes with continuous acts of sabotage along the Symplon line (an important rail line from Northern Italy to Bern, Switzerland). The few transports that did manage to get through would be blown up by more distant Partisan forces.

As events became more pressing, the Chrysler Mission was forced more than once to maneuver its main receiver-transmitter station to a safer, more concealed location.

Until then, it had been located in alternating homes and family businesses, with the last shifting to an unpretentious house in Busto, an area near Lake Maggiore that adjoined the Sisters of the Institute for the Aged, where it remained concealed and actively engaged until the end of hostilities.

Paccetti's report continued:

> It was, in fact just there, on the shores of the lake in early December 1944, that I was introduced to "Albertino" [Giovanni Marcora, a brave Partisan and subsequently Italy's Minister of Agriculture] and to Aldo Icardi. Speaking off hand, but like brothers, we embraced as if we'd been re-united after a long time. Icardi was an OSS American Italian, who had, along with many others, left his home and family to come this far in the struggle to free us from the abyss into which fascism had cast us, and store up the information passed on by our own intelligence groups. Very often in civilian clothes, he would go to check out the information himself, at great personal risk. In those few months we knew each other, I learnt to appreciate his high sense of moral-

ity as a true lover of democracy and freedom-fighter and, together with him, I'd like to thank all those friends who fought alongside us for the ideals of social justice, peace and freedom.

In other turbulent days of April 1945, Icardi effectively contributed to the surrender of heavily armed and intransigent German divisions. His authoritative and courageous intervention made possible the liberation of the area around Viarese.

For his supreme bravery and as an exemplary figure, both as man and soldier, he was awarded Italy's Silver Medal for military valor and the esteemed Congressional Medal by the United States of America.

I would like to take the opportunity here of thanking the glorious and efficient OSS for the decisive and often heroic contribution they made to the Italian Resistance, which made possible for our country to free itself with honor and to be able to declare with pride that our freedom was not given as a gift, but won at the cost of great sacrifice and blood. That it be remembered too, what behooves us and dear to our hearts, the thousands of Allies who fell and are buried in Italy and all those who gave up their young lives so that we might continue to live in peace.

Another OSS hero, Philip Frances, Medical Technician 3rd Grade, reported that the Pee Dee Mission parachuted into the 2,000 square mile, northwestern region of Liguria. It was known by the Partisans as the Sixth Zone, headquarters for two Operational Missions—Pee Dee and Roanoke.

Pee Dee's mission was to cooperate with the British Special Operations forces and the 7,000 Partisans fighting in that important area. They had been sent there to prevent Hitler's troops from retreating to Germany and to force as many of the Germans as possible to surrender.

Combined American and British airpower had become more important during the last months of the war.

At that time, January to March of 1945, there were twenty-six German divisions remaining in Italy, with less than twenty Allied divisions facing them across the front that stretched across the entire Italian peninsula, from Pisa near the west coast to Ravenna on the east.

With snow three feet high and temperatures ranging near zero during January and February, living conditions in the mountains were extremely poor. Soldiers and Partisans had to sleep on straw since there were no beds and few sleeping bags. Many other comforts had been lost as well during enemy attacks. Baths were infrequent, and even the mountain-raised men who were accustomed to such extreme conditions were susceptible to battlefield illnesses. Lice, scabies and frostbite had become a common threat, and any medical assistance was gratefully received through that particularly oppressive winter.

In late February, the Partisans launched a major attack at Mt. Alfeo in the Ligurian Alps and liberated the occupied town of Ottone, forty miles southwest of Piacenza. Following that, on April 5, the final group of Mission Pee Dee arrived at a nearby drop zone, but the airplane was forced to make three passes over the small site, with individual groups of OSS men parachuting on each pass. Medic Philip Frances was the third man to leave the plane on the second pass. Slight of build, he was tethered with another fifty to sixty pounds of equipment, mostly medicine and additional ammunition for the Partisans waiting below.

His anecdotal accounts, descending by parachute and of tending the sick are informative and engrossing:

I foolishly poured the water out of my canteen prior to boarding the plane. As soon as the green light came on, three of us pushed out of the plane door. The prop blast lifted me into the air. When my chute opened, I saw another man in front of me who had left the plane about the same time. He seemed to go down as I went up. Nearing the ground, a sudden gust of air pushed him into a tree. His chute collapsed and he fell ten feet, bumping his head on the tree. Upon landing, I ran over to give him a drink of water from my canteen but then I realized it was empty. His canteen was nowhere to be found after hitting the tree. As I cradled him in my arms, I asked a nearby Partisan for his canteen. He had been there to welcome us and pick up supplies. The Partisan passed his canteen and I immediately opened it and raised my numbed comrade's head, prodding him to drink the water as I poured a large gulp into his mouth. Suddenly he jumped up and shouted, "You son of a bitch! You're trying to poison me." When his color came back to normal I raised the canteen to my lips, quickly realizing it wasn't water but good old Italian grappa. The honor drink of all good Italian Partisans, a medicine that cures all ills.

During the next few nights, Philip's drop group was housed in a tiny alpine village, training new Partisans and spending the days demonstrating the use of 60 and 80 millimeter mortars and 50 caliber machine guns. They spent most of their time waiting for supplies that were alternately dropped at eighteen different locations in their zone of operations. Drops included arms, ammunition, clothing, food, propaganda tracts, paper for printing, gasoline, explosives, motorcycles and medical supplies.

By the time the war ended, Mission Pee Dee would receive a minimum of 115 planeloads of supplies at nineteen different drop fields.

Philip's narrative continues:

> I was the only medic with Pee Dee, unable to stay with or see all the Partisans on a daily schedule, and sometimes could not see them for at least a week.
>
> Soon after I arrived in the Sixth Zone, I met the Partisan who influenced me the most, Dr. Dolo, who was a Russian graduate of the American Medical School in Ankara, Turkey. His real name was Leopold Rumberg, and his family fled Russia in the late 30's because of persecution. Being a medic and having received only six months of combat medicine, I was very pleased to have a medical doctor for a friend. It was with Dr. Dolo who with specialist aides, saw to it that we received the great medical and dental care that was available in our zone. If injured, all Partisans, civilians, British and American soldiers were assured of immediate medical attention from a professional staff of M.D.s, dentists and nurses. A Partisan by the name of Vuccio was mainly responsible for setting up this efficient system of medical care. He was either a medical doctor or a dentist and had organized hospitals in Genoa before the war.
>
> Over the months with the Partisans, Vuccio organized hospitals and medical aid stations by converting rooms of farmhouses and making them ready for all medical uses, and recruiting a staff of ten to twelve doctors and surgeons. Farmers and civilians would work with the medical staff to provide room, food, and the day-to-day care.

He acquired needed medical supplies from American airdrops and much was confiscated from the fleeing Fascists and Germans. All this lessened pain and extended life in the area.

The Partisans, the Americans, members of missions Pee Dee and Roanoke, and all the liberated people of Italy were fortunate to have a man like Dr. Vuccio. He saved many lives. Vuccio, wherever you are, God be with you.

I will now summarize medical care required by members of Mission Pee Dee. From January 18th to April 5th, 1945, all medical care of the Americans was in the hands of Partisan doctors. After April 5th, care was provided by myself as the medic for the mission, in collaboration with the Partisan doctors. A serious head injury caused by slipping on ice, left T/Sergeant Joseph Caprioli in a farmhouse for five days where he was cared for by a Partisan doctor. T/4 George Codino had a callus removed from his right thumb on April 3rd. The sutures were removed after seven days. Seven Americans had teeth repaired or replaced by a Partisan dentist. T/5 Samuel Perusso was injured on a motorcycle fall on April 25th; however, failure to report the accident led to cellulitis on the left arm but immediate treatment with warm packs and sulfadiazine stopped the infection.

Within a few days the Partisans started the drive to liberate Genoa. As the Germans and Fascists fled northward, Partisans and Allied soldiers from many countries were liberated from various prisons.

Russian, American, British, Canadian and French servicemen, many who were airmen, were freed from the prison known as the "Casa di Studente." It felt good to be able to greet them with clothing, shoes, candy, ciga-

rettes and provide them with medical care for they had
not received any for some time. I particularly remember
one airman who was tortured by cigarette burns. The
Germans wanted a confession that he was a member of
OSS when he was not.

Within two weeks the Partisans had liberated Genoa,
as the Allied troops advanced northward into the city. The
people of Genoa had been under nazi control for over
four and a half years. The Partisans set up a prison in the
basement of Hotel Verdi for high-ranking Fascists and
Nazi officers. For some Partisans, it was time to settle old
scores, an eye for an eye. Some Americans visited the hotel
and witnessed the brutality. The leader of Pee Dee, Captain
Vanoncini, was a man of great compassion who felt that
seeking revenge in this way was wrong. Even though O.G.
members had been treated by the enemy as terrorists, not
soldiers, this meant torture or execution for many who
were captured. "Van" loved his men and could see what
might happen. He called his men together and explained
that we should not go into the basement of the hotel, or
any torture chamber. This was not the American way to
seek revenge by torture, proving to all of us that Van was
a great leader and a man of great love for all people, friend
or foe. To my knowledge, Captain Vanoncini's request was
kept by all members of the mission.

Eleven units of O.G s left North Africa and parachuted
into Southern France to assist the Maquis (French Resistance). The first unit left on June 8, 1944, two days
after the Normandy Invasion. Mission Helen, also known
as "Number 11," was the last to enter southern France
in early August 1944. My first combat medical request
came a few days later. A French farmer asked me to visit

his barn. Upon entering, I found a wounded airman whose B-25 had crashed nearby about a month ago. Upon impact, the plane caught fire and the pilot had used his hands to douse the flames, thereby burning his hair and arms. The French farmer had pulled the pilot from the plane and hid him from the Germans. Fearing the enemy, the Frenchman did not seek medical aid for the pilot. He and his wife covered the burns that were on his head and one arm form the elbow to the fingertips, with many gauze bandages. During the past month the bandages had never been removed and no antibiotics had been used. As I spoke with the American pilot, who was dressed in civilian clothes, I noticed an awful odor in the barn. I soon realized it was coming from the infected bandages. The pilots first words were, "Will you please remove the bandages." I told him that I would first need to collect some medical supplies and would return.

On my way to get the necessary supplies, I came across another medic with another O.G. mission who was passing through the area. I explained that I was looking for medical supplies to help an injured man. He told me that a lot of German medical supplies had just been confiscated. What luck! I quickly returned to the barn with the supplies.

Even though the odor was terrible as I removed the old gauze, I was determined to finish the job done and not get sick or vomit. As I got nearer to the flesh, I noticed the gauze was immersed and stuck to the flesh. I had to pull hard with the forceps to get the gauze loose. After the gauze was removed from his head, I noticed that he had lost most of the right ear and there was much infection. I cleaned the wound as much as possible and covered the head and ear areas with the sterile bandage. Upon removing the bandages on the right arm and hand, I was sure it was gangrenous and would have to be amputated. The flesh on his hand was visibly down to the bone on two fingers. I could not amputate. I knew the Allied Army would overrun the area in three or four days, and professional medical services would then be available. I gave the pilot several days of supply of sulfa drugs and asked the French family to provide the pilot with a lot of liquids and gave them Halazon tablets to purify the water. I asked that as soon as the Allied Army arrived that the pilot be removed to a hospital. I then said my farewells to the airman, never knowing his name or where he was from. He was one human being I met briefly as a medic on the road of war.

Riding in a truck for two hours, members of French Mission Helen found a few members of another mission at an abandoned mining camp in the mountainous region along the French side of the border. Upon arriving in the mining camp, Captain Fontaine placed a guard unit outside for protection against possible enemy attack. Within an hour one of the guards informed him that four men carrying something heavy were approaching the area.

Fontaine told the sergeant in charge to take the men as prisoners in order to interrogate them, and within a few minutes, four men plus one on a stretcher came into the building. They turned out to be Italian Partisans who had been attacked by Germans and could not get back to their village in Italy. It was decided between them that they should go over the mountains into France to find medical help for their wounded comrade who had been shot in the thigh that was already heavily bandaged.

Captain Fontaine did not speak Italian, leaving Philip Frances to converse with the Partisans. He informed them that he was a medic, and from what he could see, the wound was severe and the bandage had been acting as a compress. Concerned that if the bandage was removed a blood vessel might rupture, he suggested that Helen's radioman contact Grenoble for an ambulance. Captain Fontaine agreed. Questioning the Partisans, Philip asked if they had seen any Americans. They said they had seen a patrol of Americans on the Italian side of the mountains, and it was decided by all that they return to Italy with the nearby squad of Americans from Helen. Fontaine asked for volunteers and none came forward except Philip, who agreed to go with another American, Sam Perusso. He had stepped out immediately to accompany the medic.

Leaving the mining camp, the four Partisans and two Americans walked for two hours before reaching the mountain's fog covered summit. With visibility limited to only ten feet they started their precipitous descent into Italy and arrived at a plateau overlooking a small village that appeared to be abandoned.

Philip continued his description of what occurred on the way back:

> I spotted a young girl watching a few sheep and asked if she had seen any Americans. She said that the villagers and Americans had run into the woods that were about a thousand feet away. I assumed that Major Lorbeer, leader of O.G. Mission Nancy and the villagers had seen the six of us on the plateau and thought we were Germans. The field in front of the woods was treeless and covered with huge boulders formed by a glacier. I asked Perusso and the four Partisans to remain at the edge of the village. Darkness was approaching and I wanted to contact Major Lorbeer quickly. As I walked about 100

feet across the field, I removed my pistol and rifle, placing them on the ground. Then with a white handkerchief and my arms raised over my head, as if to surrender, I advanced toward the woods. I was shouting at the top of my voice, "Major Lorbeer! Major Lorbeer!" As I passed several large boulders, two men from Mission Nancy jumped out and knocked me to the ground. Upon seeing my face, I heard Dick Bruno, radio technician for the mission, shout, "Major, come down, it's Franny." After hearing my story, Major Lorbeer surmised that the small group of Germans that had been stationed on the plateau had temporarily gone to get food, clothing and supplies and that they would return by morning.

Philip's story continues with Mission Nancy remaining on the plateau overlooking the village. With orders to return to France in the morning, the men had the burden of carrying supplies, heavy weapons, Bren rifles, 30 caliber machine guns, and ammunition. An exhausting task.

When they left that morning Philip had developed a swelling the size of his fist on his right groin. Because of the swelling, Lorbeer agreed for him to walk up the mountain ahead of the group. He had removed the bandoleer of ammunition from Philip's shoulder and carried the medic's burden as well as his own. As incapacitated as he was, the stoic medic was able to keep ahead of the orderly withdrawal and reached the cloudy summit first.

Philip Frances' report ends with this fitting tribute: "The four Partisans who carried a wounded friend to safety had to be the Samaritans of all time. There was no question that these brave soldiers had thought first of their men, and lastly, of themselves."

****

There was a considerable amount of activity in the Piedmontese valleys as Partisan missions drifted off their positions along the Alps to spend time with their families. A small number of those appeared to be made up of recent deserters from the hated Fascist units and also included Russians and Slovaks who claimed they had escaped from prisoner-of-war camps. It was clear that those men lacked militaristic organization but they did seem extremely anxious to rid the world of German soldiers. As they had done with others, special men of the OSS proceeded to train these raw, but willing groups the particulars of how to handle the objectives of the Spokane and Sewanee Missions. Except for the severity of the winter weather, their tasks would have been easier than those nearer the frigid French-Italian border.

There had been no other Allied missions or radios close to the immediate area where they had parachuted, forcing the rough and ready regular crews to make a blind drop.

With the first parachuted drop the Americans immediately began to equip and train the recently formed green groups. Since most of the weapons and explosives were American or British, much of their time had to be devoted to instruction in what, to these novice Partisans, were new weapons.

Sniper fire from a fortified house had wounded several Partisans out of the hundred that had taken part in that action when the O.G. was asked, and agreed to help clean out their mutual enemy. The Germans attempted to send in reinforcements but the newly trained Partisans blocked the road, manning mortars, bazookas, and two old mountain artillery pieces. The latter proved inaccurate and ineffective, but the bazookas at 200 to 300 yards were deadly and soon knocked the roof off the house.

The Germans retreated to the cellars and used light machine guns to hold off the attack until nightfall when their snipers slipped away, abandoning their weapons and leaving four casualties.

That singular incident proved the value of any and all willing trainees and their acceptance by the Spokane Mission's O.G. to accompany them in future battles.

Major Lorbeer's responsibility was the Stelvio Pass and Bormio Partisan garrison at the foot of Route 38 that lead to the pass. Aside from an unknown number of Fascist soldiers, some 300 well-equipped German mountain troops remained at the pass with sixty soldiers. The road between the pass and the garrison was highly patrolled by white-clad German ski troopers, with a large construction dump protected by the enemy along that same road.

Allied headquarters sensed that the Germans might attempt a last stand in that highly fortified Alpine redoubt with what remained of their infantry forces in Italy. There, they could withdraw to a line at which the western end anchored at the Stelvio Pass. Allied Intelligence reported evidence that the Germans might be gathering material to fortify the area before the winter weather subsided.

From mid-March to mid-April of 1945, there was a daily exchange of fire between Partisan/American units and the enemy troops at the pass. Major Lorbeer reported:

> From our side, we used special rifles with telescopic sights, 50 caliber machine guns, U.S. 81 milimeter mortars and British 3-inch mortars. The Germans had similar long-range weapons. Distances were far too great for observably effective fire, but over a span of several weeks, the Partisans had three killed and about ten wounded. Later on, the German commander informed us that their own casualties had been two killed and four wounded, but that the firing also had caused numerous desertions, especially among Italian Fascist soldiers, who must have had the good sense to realize that the end of the war was at hand.

Partisan infantry lay in wait for retreating Germans in Florence.

On the night of March 30th, seven O.G. men and fifty Partisans raided the Stelvio construction dump at nightfall. Working their way down the steep cliffs, they swarmed over Stelvio's main highway where Partisan demolition squads blocked the road to the north and south, cutting telephone communications between the dump and the German garrisons. In the end, the main body of the O.G./Partisan raiding party finally overwhelmed the garrison guarding the construction dump and the electric cable car line that fed material to its main depository.

Two German guards were taken prisoner but most of their workers and engineers had slipped away. Large quantities of food and weapons were captured by the O.G. group, and a vast amount of materials destroyed, including 500 rolls of barbed wire and twenty tons of steel plates. Using demolition charges, the raiding party destroyed the machinery of the electric cable car system that at that very same night had been hauling materials to the Germans at the top.

It was clear that the rate of construction of enemy fortifications had been slowed to a trickle and Lorbeer's notes state in simplistic finality:

> The last week of April, a combined force of Partisans and O.G. men entered Bormio. The Italian Fascists surrendered immediately, but the German commander refused. After we threatened to open fire with what obviously were superior weapons, he agreed to leave his garrison if it was sealed up under Partisan guard rather than surrender to the American and British Army. The next day, the same German commander arrived under a white flag agreeing to the unconditional surrender of his garrison, which included a total force of approximately 300 men, together with all arms and equipment.

Overnight, the commander had learned that the entire area had already been in Allied hands. That was three days before the official end of hostilities in Italy.

As the smoke of the final day's battle cleared the Dolomites on May 2, 1945, Donovan's OSS men and their Partisan counterparts had won a resounding hurrah from every corner of a grateful world.

When all had been said and done in the Italian Campaign, records show that a total of 4,280 Allied sorties were flown, of which 2,652 were declared successful. More than 5,900 gross tons of supplies had been delivered, and 538 personnel were known to be airdropped.

Depending on their sources, statistics of this magnitude can be contradictory. But those numbers appear to be close to authentic and tend to indicate the spectacular accomplishments of the Partisans along with the Allied armies and exemplary men of the OSS.

It was noted at the Venice meeting "that with all the heroic activity of support for the Allied Armed forces that functioned in Italy, to which can be added the special operations that were joined by the Partisans, their accomplishments couldn't help but draw resounding praise from every Allied commander."

In recognition, the American O.G.s in Italy would receive the Distinguished Unit Citation, two Distinguished Service Crosses, twenty Silver Medals, ten Legion of Merit Medals, thirty Bronze Stars, twenty-five Air Medals, eight with Oak Leaf Clusters, and twenty-nine Purple Hearts.

****

A few days prior to the end of hostilities, the Germans continued fighting as though their war of aggression would never end. Their officers may have known that it was a last-ditch effort, but they didn't show it as our G.I.s continued to be targets of their sniper fire, artillery salvos and well-directed mortar fusillades.

Having spent the past six months in the frigid mountains under the worst of conditions, our battalion left those iced-over heights behind for the springtime warmth of the Po Valley. On the descent, we rubbed shoulders with thousands of other marching infantrymen emanating from every hilltop across the width of Italy.

Located on the southeastern side of the valley, the hub city of Bologna had nearly become the world-class place it is today. As Emilia-Romagna's capitol and most developed city, it was known to be one of the most significant railroad depots in Italy.

But on the day we exited the last of the Apennine slopes, I had the opportunity to view the entire city and caught a glimpse of the mangled debris that had been its famous railway junction.

All that remained were crazily twisted tracks and dangling power lines appearing as if some mischievous brat had vented his temper on a toy erector set.

It quickly became apparent that our air force had done an extremely accurate number on it. How Bologna's opulent community would ever reassemble its once glorious station mattered little to us; but today, I'm happy to know they did.

I would never know how much of that damage could have been caused by local Partisan groups, but I've been told that they did have a hand its demolition. Incontrovertible notes of the Partisan Santa Justa 9th Brigade hint of their remorseless sabotage, specifically directed at the Bologna-Porretta and Caslecchio-Vignola transit systems.

Local Partisans had confiscated motorcycles, arms, documents, police license plates and all manner of military uniforms during copious raids. The Nazi trappings would be used to disguise themselves at times when they would be most helpful.

Three hundred eighty seven actively engaged Partisans in that brigade were commanded by Pino Nucci, aided by other members of his family including, Dr. Gino Nucci, the brigade's health director, Pino's cousins and two female doctors, Busacchi and Biavati.

When in battle, the brigade's chaplain and spiritual leader, Don Gabriele Bonani, would pray for its success and safety.

Several members of the group possessed a unique talent for slinging propaganda posters onto the city's highest tension wires to flaunt their derisive blurbs on oil cloth. Unconventional attachments kept the banners in place for long periods of time, further serving to crush the ebbing morale of retreating German soldiers.

Along with these high-ranging posters the Partisans placed three pronged contraptions along the city's major routes of transport that would often delay German motorized traffic. After the enemy managed to proceed, the Partisans would place another batch in a different location farther up the highway. As a final insult to Hitler's army, Partisan squads had slashed or intercepted Nazi communications, totally disrupting the usefulness of their transmissions.

The Partisans of Santa Justa would never forget the week their hateful subjugation came to a sudden end. Clued by the high-priority order that the entire brigade return to its base in the city, they rushed down from concealed positions in the mountains and out of unsuspected hiding places around the village to comply. Allied troops had almost reached the town and the time seemed right for the brigade to make a final stand with other Resistance groups in their region that had remained actively engaged.

Although greatly reduced in manpower, straggling Nazi squads still occupied parts of Bologna and were not expected to give up easily. A concentrated Resistance effort had become necessary to aid the Allied arrival.

Key Partisan contingents were being transported back to the city in ambulances supplied by the International Red Cross. Those who spoke German wore the stolen garb of Nazi SS that would add much to the enemy's confusion that followed as they retreated.

With actions well beyond the call of duty, the fiery brigade was given its fair share of the credit for having assisted in the liberation of Santa Justa and occupied-Bologna, two days before the first Allied soldier arrived.

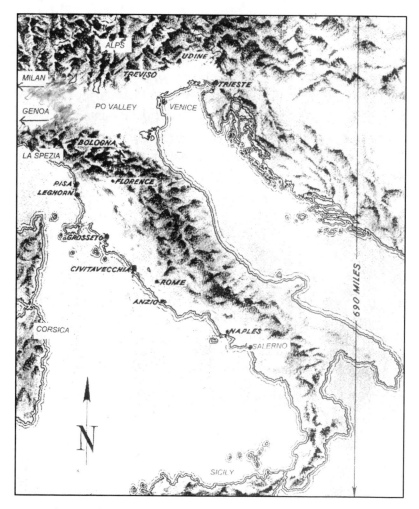

Map indicating the mountainous areas of Italy.

CHAPTER NINE

Living with the Partisans:
The Story of James Wilde

I t is immensely enlivening to fathom the crazy kind of war fought by the Italian Partisans in Italy's mountains; different kinds of battles fought in different ways. Take for example the story of a British Yorkshireman as he inadvertently blended into the tempestuous lifestyle of Partisans he befriended along the way. Ordinary Seaman James Frederick Wilde tells us of his adventures with the Italian Partisans in an autobiography titled, *The Broken Column*, first published in 1966 by George G. Harrap & Co. Ltd., and drafted by C.E.T. Warren and James Benson.

Wilde's submarine, the H.M.S. *Sahib*, had been torpedoed in April of 1943, in the Straits of Messina. The vessel stayed afloat on her buoyancy tanks long enough for Wilde and others to be taken alive by Mussolini's Italian Navy.

At that time, Italy was still part of the enemy Axis and the few captured English seamen were sent to various prisoner-of-war work camps that stretched from Italy to Germany. After one of several camp relocations, he was trucked to the 4,000 foot high mountain range near Genoa and was loaded on to a train headed north. But before reaching the Ticino Alps, Wilde managed to escape. It was there that he would link up with a band of Partisans, and to his amazement, become one of their leaders.

Allied forces were still fighting in the big toe of Italy's boot-shaped peninsula when bantam groups of Neapolitan patriots began to revolt. Brash and impulsive, their heroism might easily compare with the American Revolutionary War's Minutemen who resembled the Italian Resistance fighters with whom Wilde would ultimately bond.

Running for his life after jumping from the prison train bound for the Alps, he came across a small house fenced off from the track with underbrush, where a middle-aged trainmaster confronted Wilde and gesticulated wildly. The Englishman swung a right hook and followed with a left to the chin that stunned and dropped the loud-mouthed man.

A woman, apparently the man's wife, appeared in the doorway of the house and expressed curiosity more than anger. Wilde couldn't have known that the assault on her husband had been more than equated by her own passionate hatred of the Germans and an inherent female sympathy for this defenseless prisoner. She silenced her stunned husband, chastising him in no uncertain terms and signaled for Wilde to follow her through a yard filled with cackling ducks and chickens.

Wilde's months in an Italian prison had left him a gaunt shadow of his former self and near to collapse when he caught sight of the water tank. Terribly thirsty, he started toward it but the woman motioned him to a clump of bushes at the back of the courtyard. Wilde's legs gave way as he pushed himself to follow her instructions, crawling on all fours to where she had gestured him to hide.

He was too panicky to have been aware that the train never made a full stop, and that the information of his escape might have been passed via radio to nearby German patrols. He felt a terrible urge to sleep but the woman returned with an old pair of trousers and greasy jacket, gesturing him to change out of his prison garb. He understood only a smattering of her Italian, and in his chaotic state of mind, was too exhausted to do anything but what she bade him. After exchanging his prison uniform for the clothes she offered, she signaled for him to leave.

He forced himself to start walking again and soon found himself in the midst of vineyards and cornfields. Several farm workers appeared and he began to move toward them until he noticed three German soldiers and an Italian policeman were among them. The Italian policeman ogled him suspiciously and Wilde had no choice but to try to bluff his way through. He selected a basket at the end of a row of vines and moved slowly, as though he, too, had been picking grapes. The man in the patrol kept ogling him and conversing animatedly at the far end of a vine row. Wilde was sure his clumsiness had betrayed him.

One of the soldiers suddenly removed a "potato masher" grenade from his belt and armed it as if ready to throw. Wilde wanted to flee but his feet were unresponsive. The men's unintelligible conversation turned argumentative, and when the soldier's arm went back in preparation as if to hurl the weapon, Wilde's legs came back to life and he ran. The force of the explosion that followed knocked him off his feet, but aside from being showered with dirt, he was unharmed. He scrambled through the thick vineyards and circled back to the point where the soldiers had previously stood when he first saw them. The scheme worked. Lying prone between vines, he watched as the patrol proceeded toward a field of maize adjoining the vineyard. Wilde moved carefully in the opposite direction toward a narrow dirt road, crouching to maintain a low silhouette.

A quarter mile later he realized the reason the soldiers had become suspicious was because they observed him pick the grapes one stem at a time and not in bunches. Chagrined with his lapse of judgment, over-tired and hungry, he sought the peaceful shelter of a large chestnut tree, and after shelling and eating the fruit, nodded off to sleep.

Someone shook his shoulder and his first thought was that the enemy had found him. He opened his eyes to see a balding, slightly built Italian who was smiling at him amicably. Seeing Wilde awake, the man offered him a bottle of wine from his haversack and loudly repeated, "*Bravo, ragazzo!*" Wilde understood that much to mean "good boy."

He wolfed down a satisfying draught and was asked to follow the man who said his name was Frederico.

They arrived at a modest home where Wilde was provided with water and a towel. More at ease, he was given milk, fruit and warm bread from the oven. Then came the questions.

The Englishman told his story as well as he could in limited Italian. His host advised him that he was nearing the outskirts of the mountain village of Medassino, forty miles north of Genoa. Frederico had assured him that there he would find freedom fighters who could assist him. But since he had gained back a little of his prior strength, Wilde felt he'd rather head for the Allied lines to the south than remain in Medassino.

It was dusk when he and Frederico left the house. They arrived in Medassino where the Italian planned to leave him with a man named Pietro who had lived in America for a short time and spoke English. Frederico left, reassuring Wilde that Pietro would take him to a safe hiding place.

Pietro poured wine and for a while they chatted. He confirmed that the Allied lines were still 400 miles away, and practically impossible for Wilde to reach. During their conversation, Pietro taught Wilde the Partisan's fraternal signs, their special language and signals. Wilde also learned of the treatment given to captured Partisans and the fate of anyone found to be aiding an Allied prisoner on the run: fingernails pulled out, eyes blinded, lit cigarettes stuffed into the nostrils.

Later that evening, Pietro said his goodbyes, but not before introducing Wilde to another associate who was prepared to escort him to a safer haven at his nephew's farm.

Once in the nephew's barn, Wilde slept the rest of the night away on a pile of hay. After being awakened at dawn, he ate a breakfast of bread and coffee, and then was handed a shabby workman's cap and long-handled shovel.

The nephew led him to the edge of a vineyard and told him he was to use the spade and pretend he had been working between the vines. That night, sleep came easily to Wilde's exhausted body.

In the first light of morning, footsteps outside awakened him. Jumping to his feet, he grabbed for the shovel, the only weapon at hand. Expecting to see police or German soldiers, he was relieved that it was only a boy of about fourteen who greeted him with a lighthearted, *"Buon giorno. Sono Dino"* (Good morning, I am Dino). Wilde responded, *"Sono James."* The youngster pronounced Wilde's name as "Gems," and that nom de guerre would remain his Partisan title for the entire time he'd spend with the Italians.

Dino stayed with him all afternoon, brushing him up on the Italian he might need until he'd return in the evening to sleep in the barn. The boy's uncle, Pietro, arrived the following morning to inform Wilde that he was to stay inside as much as possible to await further instructions.

During his stay at the barn, he was told to pretend to be a mentally deficient, deaf and dumb relative who had been shunted off to the family. During that interval, he studied hard to improve his knowledge of the Italian language.

Wilde understood that he must always be in the company of the men, and when questioned or requested to show papers by Germans or Fascist police, he should behave as if he truly was truly dim-witted. That pretense would ultimately see him through a number of tight spots.

The ensuing weeks of living on the edge turned into months. American Fifth Army troops had crossed the Volturno River

(north of Naples) and the British Eighth Army had reached
Sangro (near Termoli, on the east coast), far too many hostile
miles to the south. It would take another month before the Allied
armies would have even faced their problems at Anzio and Monte
Cassino.

Wilde grew restless and made it his business to learn everything
he could of the country's language and geography. News arrived
through Pietro that the Blackshirts had left the nearby town of
San Sebastiano and that more Partisan recruits were needed to
protect the area in the event they'd return. This news sounded as
if it was his chance to become active again.

"This was it!" Wilde recalled. "No need for consideration or
debate." His civilian contact at the time was thirty-year-old
Domenico, never strong of body, yet with an urgent need to join
the Partisans. The two left for San Sebastiano to travel the five
miles of mountainous, narrow goat trails that made Wilde realize
how badly his own body was out of condition.

It wasn't long before he noticed that Domenico was a sweaty
mess, totally exhausted and not fit for mountain climbing.

Wilde would soon become intimately familiar with the region's
well-trodden mountain roads, impossible trails that could suddenly drop away to nothing. The lichen-covered paths and numerous boulders proved difficult for Domenico, but with Wilde's
help, he trudged on.

At San Sebastiano they were stopped at two Partisan-manned
roadblocks. Wilde noted, "We were greeted by polite swagger
and coarseness of tongue, a hallmark of provincial Partisans."

When they reached the village square, Wilde asked where he
could find the Partisan's leader. He was told that their brigade
and leader were both known as "Chiri-chi-chi," but that the leader
was unavailable since he and a group were fighting in another
part of the mountains. The two men were directed to a training

camp and told to get a meal at a nearby inn before being taken to the encampment. When they returned to the town square they observed groups of weary Partisans that came and left at will between the roadblocks and their posts in the hills.

One patrol of twenty men lined up and set off eastward through the small valley with two ox-carts loaded with bread and vegetables, while the rim of the piazza was lined with their civilian relatives who bid farewell to groups of young volunteers. Some were full of blustery bravado while others appeared apprehensive, licking their lips and probably wondering what they had let themselves in for. A few stood silent and impassive.

Wilde became impatient with the group's lack of enthusiasm for battle. He found a pair of heavy climbing boots and attached a sheathed hunting knife as he yearned for his chance to be the hunter rather than the hunted. The procession left the village about 5:30 that evening, taking a complicated route.

After two and a half hours of steady climbing to reach the leader's camp, they arrived at a grassy clearing nested under a rock wall overhang. Four small tents had been erected and another four were not yet assembled. Apparently most of the group would have to sleep in the open. About forty Partisans plus ten of the day's recruits squatted around a blazing fire as they ate their evening meal. Wilde and Domenico sprawled on the grass with the recruits and when the old hands had finished eating, the new men were called to get their plates filled.

Wilde spent that first night under the stars. With his jacket for a pillow he slept the tired sleep of one who really needed the rest until awakened by the sound of cannon fire in the distance. One of the older Partisans said that there was fighting in the mountains near Serravalle, a pass through which the Milan-Genoa road ran, and that it commanded the rail junction of Novi Ligure.

Wilde was amazed at the apathy that surrounded him and decided to confront the camp commander. His first question intended to be, "What are you going to do to help your men that might be at the wrong end of that enemy artillery?"

He opened the flap of the commander's tent to the surprising sight of the commander and a woman having intercourse under a ragged blanket.

The man sat upright and the woman attempted to cloak herself with the torn bedcover. Wilde offered an apology and began to leave, but the man roared at him to come back.

"Stay! Speak up! What in the hell do you want?"

The man was short but broad figured for a thirty-year-old. Everything about him was covered with body hair. The woman was about ten years younger, a sensual Italian beauty.

In his embarrassment Wilde blurted out, "I am an Englishman, and would greatly appreciate some sort of attention." As he uttered the chauvinistic words he realized how pompous he must have sounded.

The naked man shouted joyfully, "An Englishman! Bravo! Bravo! "

He shook Wilde's hand and bounced impishly around the Englishman without relinquishing it. Finally, he let go and pulled on a pair of trousers as he asked for the newcomer's history, which Wilde gave in the shortest version he could. As he spoke, the naked woman arose to dress, and did slowly and almost teasingly. For a moment, Wilde couldn't help but envy the excited commander.

The commander's enthusiasm continued, finally allowing Wilde to know he was proud of the recruiting drive he felt personally responsible for. He also provided a rambling account of recent actions in which he had taken a major part. Lastly, he told Wilde his name was Cesare.

Wilde was curious. He had heard enough of Cesare's past

from the Partisans he had met and wanted to know what in the world the braggart was going to do or say next.

Cesare then told him that Chiri-chi-chi was leading his force of about 250 Partisans near Serravalle, and had been engaged by 500-600 Germans who were supported by another 100 Fascist troops. Apparently Chiri-chi-chi's men had been causing havoc against the enemy's main trunk road, the most ambitious venture they had ever attempted, and the Germans were attempting to hit back hard.

Reports were that on the first night of battle the cost to the enemy had been about thirty vehicles and sixty men, causing the enraged Germans to counterattack in a stronger force than had been anticipated. So large a force had never been experienced, and the Partisans had to retreat deeper into the mountains. There they could take advantage of their knowledge of the terrain and disappear into the woody expanse to fight another day if necessary.

Cesare returned to the subject of recruitment. He explained that his task was to give the new men the barest amount of training, and send them to fill the gaps in Chiri-chi-chi's forces almost immediately.

At that point, Cesare stopped his explanation, stared hard at Wilde for a moment and almost shouted, "You are an Englishman. You must know all about fighting. I stand down. You are now in complete charge. Bravo!" He followed this sudden outburst by roughly shaking Wilde's hand again as if to congratulate him.

The astonished Englishman tried to explain that he was only an ordinary sailor, not even an officer, and that he knew nothing about guerrilla warfare. But Cesare remained adamant.

After absorbing this startlingly nomination, Wilde admitted to having been convinced that he might really be ready to take over. Why not? These men certainly needed better direction than they had been getting.

It didn't take long to issue his first instruction to Cesare. "Summon the men. Tell them I am in command, and I will talk with them." Not one of Cesare's men seemed surprised. Apparently they were more than ready to accomplish what they had enlisted for—fight to the death if necessary to free themselves and their countrymen from the despotism that pervaded their country.

Wilde made a point of standing tall before all the Partisans and his next order was a call to action. They would strike camp at midnight, their tents and unnecessary equipment to be left behind but well hidden. He would plan on reaching Chiri-chi-chi's force early the next day, but the rest of the present time was for instructing the new enlistees on how to handle weapons. Since most of the tyros were experienced huntsmen, it wouldn't take too much effort to instruct the few who needed it.

Finally, anyone with second thoughts about having joined up would be allowed to return home "without any reflection on their character."

About noon that day, Wilde's traveling companion, Domenico, came to see him. The man was obviously embarrassed and said he would prefer not to participate, feeling it would be better if he tried to serve in some capacity that didn't require physical strength. Wilde understood and watched as he left, hoping the man wouldn't get lost. Oddly, he felt strange with out him, perhaps the only volunteer to be returning home.

Another, the youngest of all the San Sebastiano recruits, approached the new commander, and looking as embarrassed as Domenico, begged to stay close to Wilde during the battle. Asked why, the youngster told Wilde he was afraid and didn't want the others to know. Wilde assured the worrisome fifteen-year-old that he most certainly could remain near and asked why he wouldn't prefer to go home. The boy, Eugenio, responded, "I'm an orphan and I have no real home to go back to." Wilde immediately appointed him his personal messenger.

After they were given instructions on how to handle machine guns, another eight shame-faced men decided to go back to their farms, and after they left, Wilde admonished one of the older veterans for having spat at them as they passed.

An inspection of arms and ammunition revealed an assortment of rifles, eight machine guns, twelve revolvers and fifty German stick-grenades. Aside from the revolver Wilde had previously been given, Cesare insisted that he accept one of his, a German P 38, with two clips and fifty rounds of bullets that fired the same type as the machine guns.

Before the experienced old hands settled down for a few hours rest that night they were given the details of Wilde's plan. First, he needed volunteers for an advance party, and seven men stepped forward. Wilde selected five. They would leave an hour earlier than the rest of his group to scout for enemy patrols.

If a patrol was spotted, one of the five would report back to the main body of Partisans while the other four would keep the Germans under close observation. Once the scouts reached the road to San Sebastiano they would take cover and watch for any activity along its route.

At ten o'clock that evening, the Partisans settled down to supper and Wilde tried to sleep, but the realization that this wasn't just a game made it difficult. His people were not only going to shoot guns, but get shot at as well. Some would get hit. How in the hell could he sleep?

Soon it was time to go. After the advance party left, thirty-six Partisans remained, including Wilde. He led with Eugenio, his message boy, who kept as close to him as he could. Wilde had also selected another man to accompany him who knew every inch of territory they planned to cover. The moonless sky was black, the night warm and breezeless. Occasionally they heard distant firing as they advanced, sometimes seeing long-lingering flashes in the night sky. It was apparent that they were getting closer to Chiri-chi-chi's zone.

For the first hour Wilde's Partisans stumbled along winding goat trails and rain-soaked gullies, climbing until they slipped through a narrow gap that separated two towering pillars of rock on the far side of a ridge of peaks. From there, they began descending toward the road, 1,300 feet below.

Two-thirty, a.m., they were more than halfway down and rested for a few minutes beside the ruins of a medieval guard tower. As they sat, Wilde's men became aware of a tiny glow of light as a man smoking a cigarette approached.

Freezing into silence until he drew level, Wilde stepped forward and ordered, "Stay where you are!" Before the man could speak there were cries of recognition from the men in the party. He was from Chiri-chi-chi's force.

Wilde briefly explained how he had been elected Captain, a title the Partisans couldn't be shaken from. The man said he had become separated from his patrol during a clash with a large body of Germans. The Partisans had gotten the worst of the battle and the Germans were still pouring in reinforcements that ultimately lead to their four-to-one superiority. The man was positive that Chiri-chi-chi's force would be wiped out if they fought on, and that the Germans would sweep eastward toward San Sebastiano knowing the Partisans had come from that area. "All the more reason for us to go to his aid," Wilde responded, ordering his party to follow him towards Chiri-chi-chi's location near Serravalle. An hour later they reached the paved road and located Wilde's scouts. At the same moment, they saw a line of headlights coming along the road towards them as a convoy of ten lorries loaded with enemy troops raced past their concealed position. Wilde became angry and swore. Had his force arrived a few minutes earlier they could have surprised the Germans, firing at will from their roadside hiding places. As it was, Wilde could only crouch in the shadows with his Partisans and watch the enemy speed by.

When the lorries passed, another returning Partisan came out of the darkness. He had been a lieutenant in the Chiri-chi-chi group and was able to supply more facts than the first man.

His mixed news was surprisingly good. Casualties among the Partisans had not been as originally feared; a dozen killed and between thirty and forty wounded. Chiri-chi-chi had decided that the German counterattack was so large that the time had come to retreat into the mountains, move the men south and return via a point well below the enemy forces.

Wilde reluctantly agreed that his only option was to return to base camp and wait. Having arrived back at ten o'clock that morning, he was exhausted from both the anticlimax and the physical effort, but remembering his responsibilities, saw to it that breakfast was prepared and sentries posted hourly before he fell asleep.

At noon, Wilde was awakened by the sound of a single rifle shot, a pre-arranged signal from his furthest sentries. Rushing to a vantage point, he saw six returning Partisans, so weary as to be dragging one foot after the other. They were met by several of his men who briefly explained Wilde's appointment as their leader before they arrived at his tented position. All saluted him with enthusiastic, albeit hoarse, cries of *"Capitano!"* One of the men had a bullet wound high on the inside of his thigh, which was wrapped in a dirty piece of cloth. His comrades laid him on a grassy clearing.

Wilde had little if any knowledge of how to treat the bullet wound, and fighting down the nausea, gently removed the foul smelling bandage. He tugged at the bandage causing the man to faint, which inadvertently allowed him to clean it up without worrying about causing the Partisan additional pain.

He washed the bullet wound that went completely through the thigh, glad that the smell was not from gangrene but from a lack of cleanliness endured during his trying trip. The man regained consciousness as Wilde washed his thigh, offering his thanks and telling Wilde how grateful he was. After dressing the wound with handkerchiefs and his own clean undershirt, Wilde still felt sick to his stomach but had gained an even higher status among the Partisans as a worthy leader.

The next morning Wilde conferred with Chiri-chi-chi's *Tenente* (lieutenant) who advised him not to take his new detachment back to San Sebastiano since he felt certain it was overdue for a major attack from the enemy. Instead he recommended that Wilde lead his men to a place deeper into the mountains, an area called Capannette di Pej, that was usually isolated and often used of by the Partisans. It was composed of fifteen barns, outhouses and sheds, and situated a thousand feet higher than the lower village of Pej that was 4,000 feet above sea level and southeast of San Sebastiano. The only ones who normally visited hard to reach Pej were its own permanent inhabitants.

Cesare confirmed the advice and Wilde agreed to leave with his men at midnight.

It would be necessary to best cover the distance by taking two dead- end roads. When Wilde and his men approached Pej he had expected to continue on toward the Capanette location. Nearing it, he also expected to see Chiri-chi-chi's men in some kind of encampment. Through binoculars, he saw 300 or so Partisans straggling in and around its piazza and surrounding fields.

Many appeared agitated and they seemed to be arguing with each other. Wilde's men broke from his column to join them. Amazed at the state of near panic and lack of discipline he had been observing, he asked the closest group what the shouting was about. He was told that Chiri-chi-chi's retreat southward had coincided with a full-scale German reoccupation of San Sebastiano. All now agreed that the rallying point of Capannette di Pej would probably be the next enemy target.

Whatever courage and will these Partisans previously had was gone as a frantic pessimism ruled the hour. Serious proposals being bandied about seemed mainly to focus on disbanding, dispersing into the mountains and living to fight another day. Wilde was horrified. He felt that if the Germans could be drawn far enough into the mountains it would make a marvelous gift for the Partisans. After all, this was their home territory where they could devise all manner of ambushes from which to decimate the enemy.

Wilde had yet to understand that many of these freedom fighters had families and farms that couldn't function if they were killed or gone too long. His only hope might be in setting an example by marshaling his own small group, preparing defenses and shaming most of the others into following him.

He sought out Cesare to help him put his plan into work but most of the disorganized Partisans had already gone or were preparing to leave. The former commander flatly refused, saying the situation was impossible and wished Wilde luck as he, too, disappeared with the others.

Suddenly, Wilde was completely alone. He searched for a few other members of his detachment on whom he thought he could rely, but they, too, had left. Furious, with not a single man to stay and make a fight of it, he cursed the lot as cowards.

Alone in his rage, he set off on his own on a road that led north. After a short distance he was surprised by the appearance of a sixteen-year-old lad who matched his pace. The boy said he had heard about Wilde's situation and shared his frustration. At first, Wilde's stormy frame of mind refused to respond to the youngster's plea that there was another strong Partisan leader he should visit. But the boy's enthusiasm convinced him and Wilde followed him to a nearby farmhouse where he was introduced to Gianni, a tall, bright-eyed man about his own age of twenty-three. As they spoke, Gianni let him know of his own feelings and grumbled, "Fuck them! The men who abandoned you were not real Partisans. They are only amateurs who like to pretend they've killed Fascists. But you can be sure of one thing: they left a useful pile of guns and ammunition hidden at Pej."

Gianni went on to say that he could borrow a farm lorry so that the two of them could return to Pej and help themselves to whatever equipment might have been left behind. Wilde agreed, at first thinking it might be foolhardy since his previous band of Partisans were certain that Pej was due for an attack. Yet, the idea was appealing since it represented a positive action.

It wasn't long before their lorry arrived to uncover a vast cache of machineguns, automatic rifles, German and Italian made hand-grenades and a considerable stash of ammunition.

"Now I will take you to meet some real Partisans!" Gianni said. "You will see the difference!"

As they left, he told Wilde they were going to Castagnola, the village seven miles from San Sebastiano. Wilde clutched a machine gun between his knees, feeling his mood had been helped by Gianni's description of what they'd find ahead.

Wilde took note of the surrounding landscape as they traveled. The rutty road elevated gradually for about three miles, shut off on one side by an unbroken ridge, and the opposite side by individual peaks. The road they were on opened abruptly into several valleys that varied in size, fanning out into patches of fertile land that Wilde considered as a possible access to innumerable mountain hideouts. Castagnola was situated at the junction where the valleys met, forming one major valley that was overhung on one side by an almost vertical cliff. With very few paths leading to the hamlet, only the local inhabitants had been familiar with the route and knew the way through.

Castagnola's lush main valley hugged the narrow Torbida River, its swampy tree line offering plenty of tempting opportunities for ambush, with seven lesser valleys opening to a wide range of retreat routes. The goat paths up and over the cliff face could allow those who might need it, a secret retreat away from the village. All in all, a perfect defensive site.

Wilde surmised that the village's greatest value was its commanding position for mounting an offensive, and should San Sebastiano become indefensible, this would be a perfect holding point. The top of the stony massive was known to be about four direct miles to or from the most vital German headquarters in the region.

Wilde was convinced.

The lorry rolled along until stopped by a group of excited women as they ran from a house, noisily shouting that a patrol of about twenty-four men were raiding a farm about half a mile away. Gianni immediately backed the lorry behind a wall, and without considering the odds, the two men set off down the lane on foot, light machine guns at the ready.

It wasn't quite dark and Wilde realized that they made easy targets for anyone lying in wait. While their attention concentrated on the wide ditches that edged the lane, they were suddenly jolted by the ominous sound of a hand grenade thrown from a tree. Reacting quickly, they hurled themselves into the nearest ditch as the grenade exploded, showering them with flying rocks and dirt pellets. Wilde whispered, suggesting they split up and dashed across the lane. The combination of shock and excitement of the moment didn't allow time to become scared.

He and Gianni waited in separate positions a safe range from the original grenade blast, neither of the men moving. From Wilde's position, the sight of a camouflaged German climbing down from his position in a protective tree offered a perfect target. He fired a short burst with his weapon and the man fell.

Ignoring the danger, Wilde ran to him to discover that his target was dead. Surprised that he felt no pangs of conscience at this, the first man he had personally killed, he compared it to his experiences on the submarine where firing a torpedo resulted in numerous impersonal kills.

Wilde realized that other snipers had to be nearby when he heard the sound of something metallic. Fortunately, the firing pin on the enemy's sub-machinegun had jammed, allowing Wilde time to aim and fire. He heard the man yell with pain and his first thought was that he had only wounded him badly enough to live out his life, but in his own country.

Wondering why Gianni had been silent, he saw the squad of Germans moving cautiously through the roadside trees. He aimed but was stopped short of firing when a small object came flying over his head and exploded thirty-five yards to his rear, an Italian grenade from Gianni's fruitful cache in Pej. The grenade had exploded far enough away for its shrapnel to fall short of Wilde's position, but Gianni's explosive had fallen short of the approaching Germans as well, sending them running for cover.

Wilde made haste for the lorry and quickly switched to his machinegun as Gianni continued to hurl intermittent grenades towards the trees where the enemy had dispersed.

The two men moved down the ditch, firing until the bullets from the trees had stopped, when in the distance, they caught sight of another German squad advancing in their direction. Full darkness was almost upon them and retreat now seemed the most sensible action to take before they'd be completely surrounded by Germans.

With no time to waste they rushed back to their hidden lorry to complete the trip to Casagnola. When they arrived Wilde found the village in as chaotic a state as he had found in Pej, but something had changed. Here, the atmosphere appeared to be one of swaggering overconfidence probably induced by too much alcohol. Gianni led Wilde to an inn and introduced him to a tall young man known as Primola Rossa, who was the respected commander of hundreds of Partisans in and around the village.

The three warriors supped together, and later, a real bed was found for Wilde in a nearby house. He recalls that it had a mattress, springs and laundered sheeting, something he hadn't enjoyed in a long time. Wilde reveled in that voluptuous luxury as long as he could before falling asleep.

Made aware of the Englishman's previous command, Primola Rosa placed him in charge of four of his battalions, each consisting of fifty men. Soon, the first was sent to patrol and protect a nearby mountain village, another to guard the approaches to Castagnola. The third would take on the practical duty of assisting local farmers in exchange for milk, potatoes and whatever else could be commandeered for his men. The last rested in the village and could be used as reserve for reinforcement if and when needed.

The dissemination of duties complete, Wilde expropriated one of the village schools as his Partisan barracks. The close quarters provided enough cramped sleeping-space for the men who were not on guard detail or work, or had not found sleeping accommodations elsewhere in the village.

Others managed to take advantage of personable women in Castagnola who seemed more than willing to provide companionship for the younger, lonely Partisans. Wilde had refused many such tempting offers so as not to lose the high respect needed from his men. Although, in setting a 10:00 p.m. curfew, he would not mind if some of his ardent warriors were snuggled into their own, or a lady friend's bed, so long as they didn't exceed his regulations.

One of Wilde's commands had been the use of a password, a directive that proved to be a disaster since he soon discovered that his able-bodied men couldn't be relied upon to remember it. He cancelled the order within days of its issue.

While in Castagnola, Wilde's Partisans easily visited their relatives living in or near nearby Varzi and would congregate with them whenever possible. Their conversations brought him a considerable amount of intelligence about the enemy's troop movements in that area. The latest of these, that a malevolent Fascist officer, Colonel Fiorentini, had taken hostages while in the Varzi. His list of executions included two harmless little girls whose brothers were serving with the Partisans. Such killings created a great deal of antagonism towards the Italian colonel and his overbearing troops.

One of Wilde's new lieutenants was a giant of a man known as Falco. Fiorentini's harsh treatment of the villagers had created serenity in the town when Falco suggested they take a few men on an expedition of their own to hunt for enemy troops based in the mountains. Wilde agreed. He, too, was restless, and under the cover of a moonless night they took sixty men with them.

Fiorentini's spies had informed him of the whereabouts of Wilde's Partisans, including where and when they would be operating in the mountainous area. The Fascist commander prepared an ambush. Using a doubling of his brigades that would encircle Wilde's roving platoon from two sides, the Fascist set his trap.

That night, as they confidently marched on, Wilde's squadron had been taken by surprise and pinned down by the superiority of enemy riflemen. Although the Partisans made a vain attempt to retaliate, the Fascist fire was too heavy and accurate. It would just be a matter of time before they'd be completely surrounded by the much more powerful Fascist force.

Wilde and Falco issued orders for fifty men to cease firing and withdraw as best they could through one of the two unattended flanks that appeared open to them, while the remainder of the Partisans were given the order to speed up their rate of fire. If their deception worked, it would give Fiorentino the impression that the entire force of Partisans were still locked within his ambush. At the very same time, those of Wilde's men who still remained would continue to dispense a larger quantity of firepower and very gradually retreat through the same flank the others did in a line of retreat, tempting the enemy to pursue them.

The Fascists swallowed the bait. His columns were unaware in the darkness that they were moving in a direction that would lead them to face each other, all-the-while assuming they had walled in their Partisan prey.

While the rest of the remaining Partisans were able to slip quietly through Fiorentini's trap two by two, both groups of Fascists unknowingly fired at each other from the cover of their woodsy surrounding at close range. Wilde states that he had no idea how long the carnage continued but that he could still hear them firing at each other a half hour later.

Near disaster had turned into victory since the Partisan losses had totaled only two dead and five wounded. Fascist casualties were assumed to have been enormous; among them was their leader, Lieutenant Colonel Alfieri, who died of wounds inflicted by his own men.

****

After numerous battles with the Germans and Fascists, Wilde noted that the size of enemy troops and intensity of their actions in his area had been increasing. He could only guess that German intelligence considered the zone's Partisan strength to be much larger than it really was. Although Wilde was left with a force of several hundred men, skirmishes between the two opposing forces were becoming more frequent, with the mountain-familiar Partisans invariably getting the better of their foes.

Winter of 1944-45 had arrived in the mountains and Wilde's men did their best to adjust to the extreme weather. His words relating their bitter experiences are noted here:

It was the beginning of a nightmare. Snow began to fall, a heavy, icy blanket that chilled my soul as well as my bones. I really understood now why winter was a closed season in terms of Partisan activity.

We were a large body to be operating as one unit on difficult mountain terrain, and although our men knew the point for which we were heading, the snow was swirling so strongly in the wind that it was impossible to distinguish landmarks, and even difficult to see the man in front. I felt thoroughly depressed and sick of the whole escapade. I was suffering bitterly from the cold and found myself wishing to high heaven that I was safe and warm in some prisoner-of-war camp.

The wind rose, and it seemed that, despite all the storms I had encountered at sea, I'd never really known the true meaning of bad weather. For hours at a time we battled on, each step a punishment. My feet would sink deep into the snow as though sucked in and held tight and had to be dragged free, step by step, hour after hour, and all the time the wind blew like a million needles tearing at my face, and the cold ate deep down inside me.

For some time now, my column of men had ceased to be an entity, a coherent whole, but was rather a straggling line of desperate, solitary units. They continued to stagger in throughout the night, and when morning came it was found that twenty men were missing. There was little doubt of their fate of being blown over unprotected rock-faces where the combination of wind, treacherous footholds and physical fatigue had proved too great for them.

It was almost midnight before the Partisans reached the relative shelter of the blizzard-swept barns below. They had stretched endurance and the half-dozen houses that might offer food and warmth to the limit, but all they wanted was rest.

It was now the beginning of December and Wilde's force was down to about 250 men and three women. The three were the eldest Camporotunda girls, Rosina, Giovannina and sixteen-year-old Maria. During the previous few weeks they had been acting as cooks, and their hatred for everything German was so great that they insisted on continuing to assist their "brave brothers in the field."

Wilde wondered whether they might slow down their overall speed of march, but he discovered that their standards of fitness and mountain craft were higher than those of many of his male Partisans. Despite the fact that they were wearing short skirts that usually showed uncovered legs, the three sisters remained in good spirits. Wilde was certain that their cheerfulness played a great part in keeping the general level of morale high as no man was anxious to reveal himself as less strong or less spirited than the three girls. To their great credit, none of the girls would accept any form of special treatment as they marched and climbed through the blizzard, refusing all offers of help.

As the German/Fascist cause weakened through the next few months, so did the frequency of their executions strengthen. Violence appeared to be the only outlet the enemy could substitute for their sense of humiliation and the dawning realization of defeat. They were behaving like madmen, reveling in final orgies of Italian blood.

****

Seesawing encounters ensued as the end of the war approached. And in the paragraph that follows, Wilde provides an eloquent, though brief, summary of his experiences fighting alongside the Italian Partisans in their noblest of causes :

> For me, too, it was the end of an era. It represented only a few months in my life. An episode. An interlude. Yet as I alone could know, and was not fully to realize until much later, it had been a period of my life that was to influence all others that followed. The war was coming to an end. What was done was done. Now I had to think of the future, of my return to England; even though nothing could ever be the same again.

CHAPTER TEN

Partisans Imprisoned

While on a business trip to San Francisco in 1969, my company's sales rep, Fran, introduced me to Angelo, her current beau. His rich Mediterranean accent roused my interest (I'm always intrigued by anything or anyone Italian) and after dinner I probed: Where was his hometown? How long ago had he relocated to America? All the usual queries.

Sometime during our second bottle of sangiovese, Fran let it be known that Angelo had been a Partisan and prisoner-of-war, but had flatly refused to give her any further information about his wartime experience.

"You've been there, Leon," she implored. "Maybe you can get him to open up."

Fran couldn't have been aware that P.O.W.s and battlefield veterans were usually tight lipped about their frightful ordeals and rarely discussed their war experiences with civilians. How could she possibly understand?

Before we had pulled the third cork, I'd already let Angelo know that I too had jousted with the Germans in his country and would be extremely interested in his story.

By then, I was ready to divulge my memoirs in trade for some of his. One night or one week wouldn't have been long enough to get the whole story out of him, pressing me to insinuate myself into their time together to meet him again on the following evening to learn more of his turbulent past.

Fran and Angelo couldn't have known that I had been collecting facts for this future book and any long-buried anecdotes he'd contribute could become materially important. Angelo's narrative has been assembled here from numerous scribbled notes that kept my ballpoint engaged during the flight back to Los Angeles and long afterward.

Along with scores of active Partisans and other linked civilian prisoners who had the misfortune of being seized with him, Angelo had been lucky to survive. Despite the fact that he was constantly reminded by nightmarish memories of a war that could never be forgotten, he appeared to be in good health, except for a congenital clubfoot that didn't seem to slow his gait.

Data received from Partisan organizations would often remind us that approximately 35,000 out of the 200,000 Partisan combatants had either been killed in action or butchered publicly after capture. Yet, there was no record of how many deaths occurred in slave labor camps where prisoners had been forced to hack away at the granite-laden mountains with picks and shovels until their palms and fingers hemorrhaged.

It had been many months before our attack against the hellish mountains that their digging began, never stopping until the last days of the war. Our infantrymen understood that harsh landscape too well. We had been there, done that, hoping to protect ourselves with shallow slit trenches and fox holes that stubbornly resisted every probe of our miniaturized G.I. shovels.

As we attacked the enemy's dreaded positions, it became clear that the Germans had made the greatest use of slave labor. At bayonet point, men like Angelo were forced to dig deeper and deeper into the stone-hard crests that would ultimately become the enemy's prized Gothic Line defenses. That much our battalion discovered when we opened fire against their impervious dugouts and tank traps, indestructible fortifications that could probably have withstood air and artillery attacks for an eternity.

Available records state that between the summer of 1943 and the war's end in the spring of 1945, at least 15,000 Italian slaves of both sexes had been pressed into Hitler's bargain-priced labor force.

Angelo's stirring saga tends to illustrate the generalities of what their lives were like while suffering the excessive cruelties under the onerous boots of their Nazi taskmasters. Understandably, most of the names of the German officers in charge have been forgotten, but never the experiences that reveal the helplessness of their enslaved drudges that came under the Nazi occupation.

Each had slashed away at the earth, despising every shovel full of slag they dug as they strengthened the enemy's ramparts, knowing every painful swing of the pickaxe would delay their freedom; an effort they knew would torment our infantrymen who stormed those miles of barbed wire, extensive anti-tank ditches and well-placed bunkers topped with operational Panzer tank turrets. Added to those near impenetrable barriers were thousands of well-dug-in mortars, camouflaged artillery excavations and strategically placed machine gun nests—a devilish array of fortifications that had to be subdued if our battalion was to endure. With no other choice we continued the attack—a Pyrrhic victory that was won only after 160 days of intense fighting that left our batallion with the alarming count of nearly forty percent casualties.

****

While this chapter rightfully belongs to Angelo, it will also include several other prisoners-of-war. Claudio and Francesca were just two of the unfortunate captives whose stories will unfold in this narrative.

Twenty-nine-year-old Angelo had been anything but a Fascist sympathizer, and like most of his working class associates, he despised Benito Mussolini. He had tried his best to avoid suspicion by appearing apolitical before being hauled off among truckloads of other Partisans. Almost everyone he associated with was inclined toward the political left, and one by one, had been brought to the unwilling "repentance" of what the Fascists believed to be their poetic justice.

For a while, the man's noticeable clubfoot had kept him out of harm's way until the Nazi's found out through one of their tortured captives that he had been moderately active in his neighborhood's Partisan recruitment effort.

Even with his clubfoot, the limping prisoner had made an immediate impression on the camp's German captain. No sooner had Angelo stumbled down the truck's tailgate when Captain Richter noticed his handicap, and needing a go-between, appointed him to be acting corporal of the seventeen other inmates he arrived with.

After Richter's lieutenant collected the watches and wallets they had confiscated "for the fatherland's mounting war demands," he allowed Angelo to keep his inexpensive wristwatch to maintain the daily work schedules.

The truckload of captives were led to their cold and gloomy quarters in a cave that had previously been dug out of a mountainside by previous prisoners when Captain Richter moved closer to Angelo and muttered in school-learned Italian, "Handle these men right and you will be rewarded with extra food and cigarettes."

His words sounded like a warning in their presentation, Richter letting Angelo know he was deadly serious. Thrusting the business end of his Luger into Angelo's ribs he hissed loudly enough in a fusion of German and Italian for all to hear: "You will do as I say, no? *Alles schnell! Capisce?*"

The captain lingered long on each word, emphasizing each syllable by shoving the barrel of his sidepiece harder into Angelo's rib cage. Its sharp gun-sight burned the message into Angelo's torso but he dared not complain.

Not too many days prior to his capture, Angelo had been a foreman at a furniture plant, used to giving, instead of receiving orders. When he gave an order he said it firmly, but with consummate tact. Now, the shoe was on the other foot and he hated its fit. The other prisoners empathized with Angelo and implicitly considered keeping their Italian brother out of trouble. Sure, they'd make an effort to accept this lame-footed corporal's orders, keep the grumbling down to a minimum, try not to make his life any more miserable than their own.

Under most circumstances, the intrinsic nature of prisoners was to resent anyone that had assumed power over them, especially one from their own group. Angelo sensed their misgivings and vowed to let them know that he, too, shared their hatred for this enemy, and would do what he could to retain their esteem. But he hadn't yet heard what it was he'd be responsible for.

On the truck from Rome, he and other prisoners revealed shreds of their past and Angelo never forgot one older man's story. Claudio had worked as a bank officer and had covertly distributed anti-fascist propaganda tracts to apartments in his neighborhood. He and his wife, Francesca, had been forcibly routed from bed one night when they were awakened by the sound of rifle butts bashing against their front door. Opening it, Claudio was startled to see a squad of German soldiers, their leader barking at the terrified elderly man to back away as the squad entered the apartment.

Unable to ask why, Claudio and his wife were forced at gunpoint to obey the officer's brusque order to get dressed. Feebly complying, they could only watch in dismay as their apartment was being pillaged of its costly accessories by the major's brash soldiers.

Francesca's hysterical cries were meaningless and her wailing fell on deaf ears since none of their neighbors dared open a door to see what had brought on the unusual ruckus. The couple were marched down three flights of stairs in a state of disarray, tripping over their untied shoelaces to the piazza below where a caravan of trucks waited, most already loaded with cowering passengers.

By that point in time, Father Benvenuti had become used to such midnight interruptions, and being used to these raids the good priest had made it his business to oversee these midnight roundups, but could do little to slow the coarseness of the SS.

Claudio and Francesca were shoved past the first two trucks that blatantly displayed chalk-marked Stars of David and the appellative "Juden," which malevolently advertised the ethnicity of prisoners it would haul.

Claudio shuddered and crossed himself. For those few seconds he was pleased to have at least avoided the unenviable fate that lay in store for those Jewish prisoners. At first, he too had been suspected of having Hebrew blood, but his priest had audibly vouched for Claudio's distinguished participation in church activities when he and Francesca were brought down to the dark street.

Fortunately, Father Benvenuti had been present when the German officer stopped at the first van. Had the SS officer ignored the priest's urgent appeal, Claudio could have been trucked to a jam-packed boxcar headed for a Jewish death camp.

Francesca became hysterical as she was forcibly wrenched from the company of Claudio, and pushed aboard another tarp-covered personnel carrier that had already been partially filled with weeping, wild-eyed women. They would be traveling separately to some unknown destination. Claudio sniveled pitifully but could only watch helplessly as her truck pulled away.

Thinking back, he realized too late that those seemingly harmless political discussions over lunch with men he thought of as close friends had been the cause of his arrest, especially one who had been his assistant. Most likely, the man had been a covert Fascist sympathizer who was desirous of nabbing his boss's job as head cashier, and Claudio blamed himself for not being careful enough to conceal his political bent. Caught in the net of the hard-hearted SS, all he could do was to brush the wetness from his eyes with his shirtsleeve, and pray like he never had before.

Claudio was the oldest of Angelo's crew, and even in his salad days, had never once been forced to sleep in penetrating dampness. The claustrophobic cave that served as his new dormitory reeked badly of latter-day farts and stale tobacco smoke.

Unaware of where Francesca had been taken, he was gravely concerned for his wife's safety, a worry that would haunt him every day of their separation.

Claudio's hands had begun to tremble, making it difficult to clasp even the daily cup of weak coffee that came with a breakfast of slushy, unfamiliar porridge. It took all ten fingers to keep the aluminum beaker from spilling. This he was afraid to admit openly since Captain Richter might send him to join the death-bound Jews to get rid of him. As a bank officer with little time for physical exercise, his muscles had become flabby, all of which didn't help in the hard labor that was forced on him in the camp. Since the terrible night of his seizure, the sharpness of his intellect had begun to suffer as well. The man made valiant attempts to retain his cutting edge to keep his keen sense of reason from failing. Stolen minutes found him reading anything printed in German, such as labels and paperback books he'd manage to acquire from a guard. These he'd attempt to interpret, one word at a time, without the necessity of comprehending a single story line.

During our dinner-table conversation in San Francisco, Angelo echoed the deep-seated feelings familiar to every prisoner-of-war. "A section in our maddened brains kept us going," he said, "hoping and praying that Allied soldiers would get to us before our bodies gave out. And that day, when America entered the war, we became even more impatient and asked ourselves, 'When, damn it? When? How soon?' I'm sure that's what kept a lot of us going."

For reasons I discovered later, Angelo seemed to derive pleasure when he talked about Claudio. "The old man's destiny seemed limited to endlessly pick away at the rock hard mountain, hoping to live long enough to see his Francesca again. Like all of us, his entire being rebelled at the thought of digging Hitler's goddam bunkers deeper, the war longer. Shit! We all felt that way! Chipping away bit by bit at the friggin' clay, the build up of beet-red blisters made even the little that Claudio was capable of more frustrating. I watched him get frailer by the day, and as much as I wanted to, I couldn't do a damned thing to help the old guy."

At least two armed guards were always posted at the entrance of the cave that Angelo and his men had scoffingly named "The Ritz." Escape was out of the question. Even the outdoor toilets they had hastily dug were protected with barbed wire and a guard. Not a chance anyone could sneak away.

As the summer progressed, a tin cupful of watered down bean soup and a sliver of dark brown bread made do for the prisoners. Even the guards complained that their rations were getting scarcer. Unforeseen problems near Stalingrad had seen to that.

Angelo's men had to be abruptly awakened to work at near dusk.

"Get your asses up!" Angelo would holler at his drowsy crew. "You don't want the lousy Krauts to cut off my *coglioni*!" Always attempting to put a touch of good humor into his commands, he'd often add, "If the bastards do, I'll make you eat the damned things if we're late!"

Just before nightfall, the Mercedes-Benz pick-up van was due to arrive in time to take Angelo and his crew to the dig. Any other daylight time would be foolhardy since they'd be open to Allied air attacks.

"Work at night, sleep when and if you got the damned chance by day, unless the sky was dark because of rain," Angelo said. That was the general rule.

Only a few months earlier Italian laborers had been treated like humans, hired as men, not slaves, paid almost equitably for their day's work. Then everything changed. Times were getting tougher for the retreating Germans and Deutschmarks were becoming harder to come by after Hitler's *putsch* in Russia. Berlin was pressed to grab whoever and whatever it could from wherever it could, and damn Clausewitz's Rules of War.

Der Schicklgruber prayed to his pagan deity, pleading for his scientists to complete the formula for the atomic bomb and pushing them beyond the limit. But the best of Germany's scientific academia had been Jewish physicists, and fearing for their lives, many had wisely left for less threatening places to work and live.

As time passed, Angelo's slave-mates had become more uncommunicative and self absorbed. Why tell jokes? What the hell was there to talk about? Any horsing around could only be minimal at best.

When the skies became dark enough they would be transported to the mountain where the digging was to be done. Each man was handed a pick or shovel off the quartermaster's truck that was parked on the rutted, steep road they had previously chopped from out of the impermeable Apennine earth. From there, they would march single file to the site where construction of the trench or gun emplacement was underway.

Under the watchful eyes of malevolent guards, they'd hack gaping excavations out of the rocky ground until the phosphorescent hands on Angelo's wristwatch showed it to be the witching hour. Forty-five minutes before sun-up. Only then could they leave the hateful project while it was still dark enough to avoid being seen by nosy Spitfires.

As it was with other slave laborers, Claudio's excruciating pain meant little to the hard-driving Austrian engineers in charge of the digs.

"Put your damned backs into it! Another half meter over there! Move!" An occasional rifle butt emphasized the need for some poor drudge to push himself harder or risk an even more painful future. If one of the crew didn't respond quickly enough, poor Angelo would also suffer by being denied his larger slice of bread, or his weekly allotment of two packs of German cigarettes. Fear for the loss of those priceless luxuries had occasionally put him in the loathsome position of exercising strict control on his men, which ultimately led to his becoming something of an outcast. Although he said he did his best to avoid it, he was spurned by nearly all the prisoners, a distressing predicament he hated..

The Guard reminded him that it was 4:15 a.m. Angelo signaled the nearly exhausted men that it was quitting time.

"To the trucks, *amici*!" he yelled, doing his best to sound amiable.

****

Earlier that night, the men had hit a particularly rocky vein and Claudio was barely able to move. His shovel reverberated as it clanged against stone, and the resulting blisters on his palms leaked blood and discolored lymph.

His long-handled spade proffered the gory results of sitting behind a desk too long. Hunched over and cursing in agony, he threw the tool down in disgust. The nearby Todt engineer and a

German guard muttered harsh sounding words to each other he couldn't understand. Claudio could have easily cried at that moment, mostly from the stinging pain that cramped his back and shoulders and gnawed at his fingers. Angered instead, he doused his hands with what little was left of his drinking water to cleanse the wounds before joining the others who had already boarded the truck. Rest and a luxurious peace at the unwholesome Ritz was the relief he looked forward to. A couple of hours of sleep had been the necessary escape from hell.

Aboard the van, Angelo looked closely at Claudio's hands and gasped. "I'll talk to Richter about giving you the day off tomorrow," he said, "but don't count on it my friend."

"I would be most grateful," Claudio responded, surprised at Angelo's concern. It wasn't like any man in his position to stick his neck out unnecessarily.

After Angelo filed his report the next morning, Captain Richter entered the cave and requested that Claudio present himself, then made a cursory effort to inspect Claudio's wounds. Repulsed by the sight, the officer instructed Angelo to have Claudio report to the mess sergeant with instructions that he was only to do temporary kitchen duty.

"His hands can use all the soap and water they can get. And I'm sure our cook will make proper use of him for as long as necessary, but no more than three days. And by the way, this place stinks!" Richter grimaced. "Who in the hell shit in here?"

Angelo wouldn't dare answer. Having been restricted to the confines of the cave, he and the men had almost become accustomed to the rank mix of odors, particularly the flatulent smell of improperly fed, outraged stomachs that insisted on breaking wind whenever relief was needed.

The days came and went. During the rest of his time in the camp, Claudio's hands continued to ulcerate, a minor annoyance to Captain Richter who would occasionally allow him another few days relief in the kitchen.

****

Ten kilometers to the north, Francesca had also been toiling in the kitchen of a rear echelon German command post near Firenzuola, high up in the Apennine chain of the Gothic Line defenses. Recoiling from the daily drudgery at first, she did her best to accommodate herself to routines she had rarely bothered with in the past.

Shortly after the war, details of Francesca's imprisonment were imparted to Angelo when he and Claudio had become lasting friends. She could never forget the dreadful humiliation of that first day in her new quarters and forever etched in her memory.

All eighteen sobbing women had been indelicately handled as they clambered down the truck's tailgate, frightened out of their wits at what might happen next. The long, bumpy ride from Rome in what Francesca later referred to as "a cattle car," left them disoriented, exhausted and chilled to the bone when they arrived at the enemy's encampment.

The sniffling women cursed quietly, afraid to be overheard. "Bastards. Thoughtless pigs."

Almost immediately upon setting foot in their prison camp, a squad of soldiers directed them into an old, run down barn. Once inside, the women gestured to make their toilet needs known, and were finally permitted to relieve themselves in an outhouse that held a single discolored aluminum sink and a two-holed, wooden toilet plank, all reeking of powerful antiseptic.

For women like Fancesca, urinating in the company of others was an embarrassment she'd have to learn to live with. The first of many humiliating conditions meant to bring her down to the commonest of levels.

The barn and its surroundings stank of animal dung and DDT powder that had been dispersed too freely. A lieutenant pointed to piles of loose straw that had once been fodder for livestock that no longer existed. "You will sleep here," he ordered in faltering Italian, then dutifully added, "beds will come in a few days."

Apparently incomplete, the camp had been one of recent confiscation, and in the dim light of a single forty-watt bulb, the women watched in dismay as rats scampered freely across the overhead beams, unaffected by the whitish powder that had been sprinkled below.

Sleep had been next to impossible and would come only in spurts. At 5:00 a.m. the same lieutenant arrived, barking loudly at the sleepy women. "Up! Everyone get up! There will be an inspection by the *Kommandanten* in forty-five minutes!"

Their purses had been removed early on and only a small toilet kit containing a comb, brush and sanitary napkins had been made available to them during their tedious ride. With the least amount of effort given their hair, they brushed the straw off the clothing they had slept in and lined up in the cold dawn air at the outhouse. With barely enough time to urinate, they timidly awaited the commanding officer in the barn. He strode through the doors at exactly 5:30, appearing to be the comically cinematic type of officer they had seen in films.

"*Achtung!*" the lieutenant shouted, clicking his heels and snapping into attention. Then, to quiet the complaining women, he yelled, "*Silencio*," directing them to make a single line facing him.

The major studied the quieted women for a few minutes, as did Francesca. Two of them might have been streetwalkers, she thought, since their garb and attitude hinted of a more flamboyant past.

The major spoke in hushed tones to his aide who had been taking notes, demanding the name of each woman as they passed, comparing and checking it with his manifest. Satisfied, he left the lieutenant and his aide to finish the task.

Names of five women were then called out by the lieutenant to be transported to the laundry facility at seven o'clock the following morning and report for duty to the person in charge.

The names of the next seven were called, and told they would be taken to the kitchen at 5:00 a.m. to assist the mess sergeant in charge and do whatever he might need them for. Francesca was included in that group.

The six remaining women, among them the two harlots, were told they should be ready to leave as soon as transportation became available.

Francesca noticed that those six had been the youngest of the passengers on the truck. Obviously, she and the other dozen women were older, somewhat heavier or plain-featured, and presumed that the sexier six were the most likely to be appreciated by higher officers residing in the safety of the rear echelon. The major's future promotion and advancement in rank might rest on his superiors knowing he was thoughtful enough to have consigned the young ladies for their various pleasures.

Four years younger than her husband, Francesca's figure displayed palpable signs of becoming less shapely than it once was. She loved that Claudio didn't mind, calling her "pleasingly plump." As yet, Francesca hadn't considered the thirty pounds she would lose in the stockade's hostile environment.

The sun hadn't quite made it over the mountain on that first day. Francesca found that her kitchen duties consisted of doing everything except cooking. The corpulent Austrian chef and two assistants were adept enough to tend to the meals, but more menial chores were Francesca's lot. Picking at the rare, leftover tidbits after the soldiers ate was a definite no-no, but with the aid of the permissive mess sergeant's myopia, she occasionally enjoyed the scraps the men had not eaten.

Her main tasks were to peel potatoes, sweep and wash the floor, scrub the oversized aluminum pots, set and clear tables, then remove the garbage.

Francesca and three other women would serve the higher officers in another, smaller mess hall where they usually dined by candlelight. To her, it was as if they were in some fine restaurant in Berlin. The officers would never eat in the same room with the lower ranks. It wouldn't do for the simpler underlings to witness the more wholesome fare their chieftains occasionally received.

Working conditions at this midway station were tolerable when compared to what she had heard from the women who worked in the laundry. Realizing that her situation could have been much worse, she was grateful that she had been given the best of the degrading options left to her as a prisoner and prayed every night that wherever he was, Claudio might be treated as well as she. Unfortunately, he wasn't.

****

It was almost a year and a half later that all prisoners would rejoin their former lives, however changed. Their agonizing existence till then had been anywhere the Germans needed to set up defensive positions: northern Italy, the Dolomites, Brenner Pass, or as far away as Germany.

When Field Marshal Kesselring was finally forced to surrender and the Allied unifying agency at last brought husband and wife together the former prisoners shed unrestrained tears of joy.

Claudio weighed forty-two pounds less than he did when he had been taken prisoner. Francesca had sprouted more ash-gray hair and almost slimmed down to her pre-marriage weight, but he'd have to get used to the unfamiliar dark shadows under her eyes that mirrored the nightmarish humiliations she had suffered. The circles they made would remain for the rest of her life.

More fortunate than many of their perished brothers, the couple was thrilled to still be alive to resettle in Rome. Although Italy's economy would take time to recover from the ravages of war and enemy occupation, Claudio managed to find work in another branch of his former bank. But the scars on the palms and fingers of his hands, along with the arthritic pain he had suffered, remained a constant reminder, especially when using calculating equipment.

Angelo and Claudio had grown close, their lives inseparable until the Angelo left for America when Claudio passed away in 1961. Francesca remained in Rome and the two often corresponded.

Angelo told me that he had learned to be less impulsive and had softened during his stint as the enemy's pseudo corporal. The soul-searching months of suffering had made him more pragmatic and allowed him to give up his past livelihood of fabricating furniture frames. Rather than repeat the complications of being in business for himself, he became a sales representative for other furniture manufacturers he had done business with. His territory was the entire United States, where his employers correctly considered his delightful Italian accent to be an asset.

Angelo kept in touch with Fran, but I lost track of him during his travels. Fran notified me later that he had passed away from a cancerous pancreas in 1992, at the age of seventy-seven.

CHAPTER ELEVEN

Of Men and Madness

The Location: Tuscany and the mountains.

The Situation: Allied gains in Europe and the sting of recent Partisan successes in Italy were taking a heavy toll on the Germans. It had become obvious that Allied troops were closer to victory when Tuscany's innocent citizens became Hitler's unwilling scapegoats. Berlin's frustrated leaders assumed that a stronger approach would turn the tide of aid and affinity away from the Partisans and orders were sent to suppress suspected villages with heavy-handed persecution. Nazi field-officers immediately carried out a progression of merciless atrocities against the peasants, their women and children, even nursing babies. The blood of innocents ran in the streets of sleepy towns and villages throughout Italy.

From Arezzo in the south, to Lucca and Pistoia in the north, der Fuhrer's mignons of death adopted the countenance of the Grim Reaper. Eyewitness reports follow, telling of the savage hunt during which the Nazis murdered a totaled of 4,461 civilians. From one province to another, village laymen told of wholesale massacres; babies that were finished off with daggers, others killed with butcher-hook hangings and countless women raped. This, all in the path of the slow German retreat toward each line of defense.

Manciano, in the province of Grosseto, happened to be one of the first Tuscan towns liberated by the Allies. Because one of its outer districts had been retaken from the enemy by a strong group of Partisans at first, worry among the civilians mounted. They knew that severe retribution usually followed whenever Partisans achieved success. The Manciano reprisal came in the form of a sweeping directive in which Marshal Kesselring issued an onerous order. "The fight against Partisan bands and their sympathetic peasantry," he decreed, "must be conducted with all available means and with the most harshness." His soldiers willingly obeyed. They had been well trained and the terse message was crystal clear.

With Allied infantry snapping at their heels, and undiminished pressure applied from their impatient commander, many officers of the Wehrmacht lost sight of any human compassion they once may have had.

Battalions of Nazi 16th SS Division German troops had been harried from all sides and began a series of sadistic acts as they introduced their new plan of terror in the vicinities of Arezzo and Florence. On the 29th of June, in the commune of Bucine, seventy-four inhabitants were randomly selected to be their first victims. Following that wholesale carnage, another 161 were massacred in the area of Civitella della Chiana.

Inexorably, the resolve of the Partisans became increasingly anger-driven as they continued to harass their German and Fascist enemies. In retaliation for the heedless butchery the Partisans launched a surprise attack in which the Germans suffered many dead and wounded. The battle continued when the Partisans captured a Fascist headquarters in Pian d'Albero. About fifty Partisans took possession of a large Albero farmhouse after a bitter fight. Afterward, twenty-one Partisans and several members of the farmer's family were taken prisoner by the Germans in an

Captured Partisans were often hung by hooks embedded under their jawbones or shot and displayed in town squares for the villagers to see.

early morning counterattack. They were hanged from crude scaffolds like freshly butchered meat with a large, pointed hook deeply implanted under their chins—an oft-used method to serve as a warning to all nearby villagers: See and think twice about aiding the Partisans.

But the hardening of Partisan motivation and an increase in their exploits after each civilian purge, forced the German field marshal to suggest another plan which he sent to Berlin for acceptance. His plan would minimize the increasing intensity of Partisan retaliations and his own mounting casualties, a divergent idea that was immediately vetoed by Berlin.

Soon after the rejection of Kesselring's plausible suggestion, the commune of Cavriglia suffered renewed carnage, where at dawn, seventy-three people were unmercifully machine-gunned in the square. Still not satisfied, the German captain in charge of that operation permitted the savagery to continue by ordering his soldiers to throw gasoline on the bodies, then set them on fire.

Not long afterward, another 250 innocents were added to the growing numbers of the enemy's atrocities. They had been merely seeking refuge during their exodus into the protection of the nearby mountains but were captured and machine-gunned as they approached the first rise.

Unlawful acts against humanity continued to the very end of the war in many communes. Most notably, when the Germans forced 560 civilians into the town's churchyard in Sant'Anna di Stazzema and massacred them by machine gun. Those who still had breath in their bodies were finished off by an officer's pistol.

The tragic history of that village was made into a fictionalized Hollywood movie titled *Miracle at Sant'Anna* in 2008, a Spike Lee film that tells the story of four black American soldiers who get trapped in a Tuscan village during WWII. It seems it was scripted by a writer more interested in dramatic entertainment than facts, The truth regarding the infamous massacre that included most of Sant'Anna's women, children and elderly still remains deeply etched in the minds of descendants that now reside elsewhere. Very few progeny remain to remember the nightmare of what had once been a quintessentially charming hilltop town in Tuscany.

A metal cabinet in Rome's military court contains accurate eyewitness notes of the atrocities committed. Today the town endures, partially rebuilt and minimally occupied as a memorial to its dead; its historic name recalling the scene of one of the most egregious war crimes to be perpetrated on Italian soil.

The slaughter at Sant'Anna was ultimately ascribed to Waffe-SS officer Walter Reder, of Himler's hated 16th SS Armored Infantry Division, described as an act of revenge against the Partisans who were operating in the province of Lucca.

With advance knowledge of the German plan prior to the day of butchery, a handful of heroic Partisans who resided near Sant'Anna vainly attempted to do battle against a much larger force of German infantry. Realizing beforehand that their attack was suicidal they managed to take a heavy toll on Reder's men before they, themselves, were shot and killed.

On August 12, 1944, German SS troops of the 2nd Battalion, under the command of SS-Haupsturmfuherer Anton Galler, had been moving in four columns towards Sant'Anna, arbitrarily committing atrocities along the way. Galler's soldiers hadn't yet reached Sant'Anna when he marched through the pastoral cantons of Mulino Rosso, Capezzano di Pietrasanta, Franchi and Pero, with weapons blazing. Whoever couldn't flee those unfortunate hamlets were quickly disposed of with the bullets or double-edged bayonets. In nearby Vaccareccia, the storm troopers trapped seventy civilians in a stable, decimated them with hand grenades and machineguns, then covered up the gory mess with flame-throwers, virtually cremating the entire village.

Finally arriving in Sant'Anna, Commander Galler's tank grenadiers forced the town's terrified inhabitants into a walled-in area in front of the town's church, trapping them into an insurmountable barrier from which they couldn't escape. With the swelling volume of hysterical prisoners packed into the church square, Galler radioed Commander Reder, who, in turn, contacted Berlin by phone for permission to proceed with the slaughter. Within minutes, approval was given and the storm troopers did what they had come to do. The village's desperate priest begged for mercy and cried out in vain. He, too, lay lifeless among the torn bodies.

It was noted by several concealed onlookers that after the crowd had been raked by machine guns, the German commander appeared to derive pleasure from each coup de grace he delivered. All the bodies were then stacked by German soldiers and burned. That infamous "scorched earth" example was meant as a warning to other towns that dared assist Partisan freedom fighters.

Among the 560 dead were 116 children. The youngest victim was later identified as only twenty days old, the oldest, eighty-six. That horrible deed served only to further inflame Partisan brigades, much to the regret of the Germans they would encounter during later battles in the northern provinces and mountainous country to the north.

Much of the Sant'Anna narrative was offered to us by the eminent correspondent in Florence, Signore Claudio Biscarini, an author in his own right and specialist in the collection of military records and their documentation.

His office is officially called the Centro Di Documentazione Internazionale Storia Milatare. In the following letter, he is responding to questions he received about the afore mentioned Hollywood film, *Miracle at Sant'Anna*:

At Sant'Anna of Stazzema, the morning of August 12, 1944, soldiers from the 16th SS Panzer-Division surrounded the town and killed more than 400 people.

The official number of dead is 560, but some military scholars have affirmed that, in reality, the number is insufficient, and should have been more than an additional 100. The town of Sant'Anna, in reality, is formed by a series of small cantons, located in the mountains that dominate Serravezza and the Versilia. To arrive at the square where the church is located and where so many were killed among old people, women and children, still today there remains a narrow hilly street. In the area, in 1944, there were Partisans, but on August 12, most had been already transferred to another place.

The massacre was not caused by any treason of the Partisans, (as the movie intimates) and not even for the presence of Partisans, but as it happened in other parts of Tuscany, from the fictitious necessity of the Germans to keep clear their lines of communications to make a bridgehead along the Gothic Line without being burdened by the Partisans and their civilian supporters.

This, in summary, is the true story and without any historic foothold, apart from the fact that in the film, the 92nd American Division did fight in Italy. To give an example, one of the black American soldiers goes to the attack on the river Serchio, holding in a net at his side the head of the statue Primavera that is found on the bridge of Santa Trinita in Florence.

Now, as you probably know, when the Germans exploded the bridges in Florence the nights of the 3rd and 4th of August in 1944, the four statues on the Santa Trinita bridge were also destroyed except for a few fragments. After the war the bridge was reconstructed as it was before the war with all the original materials and fragments that were able to be recovered. The head of the Primavera was missing and then found in 1962, as I remember, from a worker on the shores of the Arno River and put back in its place. What officer or soldier would have gone on fighting with a souvenir of marble equipment weighing at least 30 chili (66 pounds) attached to his leg?

Always at your disposal, cordially, Claudio Biscarini.

****

On June 22nd, 2005, after a yearlong trial, Italian judges in La Spezia convicted former members of the Nazi SS who were accused of taking part in the massacres, and sentenced them to life imprisonment in absentia. The defendants, by then, were all over eighty years of age. Although a new trial has been requested in modern Germany, the age of the accused and their distance from Italy has, so far, spared them. None of the accused has had the moral conscience to confess, even though they were aware of having immunity.

Ironically, on the day this chapter is being written, December 9, 2010, it has been reported that a court in Munich, in one of Germany's last major Nazi war crime trials, jailed a ninety-year-old former German army commander for life for having ordered a massacre of Italian civilians in 1944.

There are many such harrowing stories of atrocities that have been recorded. For example, the incident in which German soldiers forced eleven males aged between fifteen and sixty-six into the ground floor of a farmhouse and then blew it up, but only the youngest, Gino Massetti, survived to suffer his serious injuries. Six decades later, Massetti, now in his eighties, testified during a previous trial.

Josef Scheungraber was the only officer from a company of soldiers who carried out the murders, claiming it was in retaliation for an attack by Partisans that had killed two of his German soldiers. Scheungraber, who was the commander of *Gebirgs-Pionier-Bataillion* 818, a German mountain infantry battalion, had been charged with fourteen counts of murder and one of attempted murder. At his trial, though hard of hearing and walking with the aid of a cane, he defiantly wore a traditional Bavarian jacket as the verdict of guilty was pronounced. The prosecution had demanded a life sentence for Scheungraber, who had spent decades since the war in the small Bavarian town of Ottobrunn, running a woodworking shop and taking part in marches in memory of fallen Nazi soldiers. His defense attorneys have said they will appeal the sentence. For now, Scheungraber remains a free man, despite having been convicted in absentia by an Italian military tribunal, in September 2006, and sentenced to life imprisonment. To date, he has never been to brought to justice because Germany does not extradite its citizens without their consent. His trial was expected to be one of the last cases dealing with atrocities of the Nazi era.

"For sixty-five years we have been waiting for truth and justice," the village's Mayor Andrea Vignini stated. "Many of the victim's families had moved away from the town [Sant' Anna] because they could not bear the memories of the massacre."

RESOURCES

Due to the close kinship I shared with Italian Partisans during and after World War II, I was successful in acquiring many of their documented actions and obliged to narrow them down to representative narratives presented within the previous pages. Almost all were from early pertinent histories that were tendered without copyright, but all were gratefully offered with Partisan or historian permission, such as those included in the bibliography that follows. Many were donated by the offices of ANPI (Associazione Nazionale Partigiani d'Italia), and to a greater extent by Signore Claudio Biscarini, who is in charge of documentations at Centro Di Documentazione Internazionale Storia Militare in Florence, Italy. Signore Biscarini authored many historic military books, several of which are noted below.

Siena 1944: Guerra e Liberazione. Claudio Biscarini and Vittorio Meoni

Lido Duranti: Vita di in Partigiano Ucciso Alle Fosse Ardeatine. Claudio Biscarini and Savino Ruglioni

Battaglione Reder: La marchia della morte. Submitted by Claudio Biscarini

Da S.Anna di Stazzema Alle Fosse del Frididio: Agosto/ Settembre 1944. Submitted by Claudio Biscarini

Glie Americani e La Guerra:Conveno internazionale di studi storici. Notes from the international convention of OSS & Partisans in Venice 17-18 October 1994

Montopoli 1940-1944: Il Passaggio della Guerra Nei Documenti Italiani, Alleati e Tedeschi. Claudio Biscarini, Luciano Niccolai and Fabrizio Mandorlini

Fronti di Guerra: Di Storia Militare. Claudio Biscarini

L'Estate del '44: L'eccidio del padule di Fucecchio. Riccardo Cardellicchio

Torri e Cannoni: Il passaggio del fronte a San Ginignano. Claudio Biscarini

Guerra in Val D' Arbia: Comune di Monteroni D'Arbia. Claudio Biscarini and Gino Civitelli

Powder River: 91st Infantry Division. Roy Livengood (Turner Publishers, out of print)

Thunder in the Appennines: The Story of the 361st Infantry Regiment in Italy. Roy Livengood

History of the 36rd Infantry. Captain Ralph E. Strootman (Washington Infantry Journal Press)

The Broken Column: The Story of James Frederick Wilde's Adventures with the Italian Partisans. C.E.T. Warren and James Benson (George G. Harrap & Co., Ltd.m, 1966)

The O.S.S. in Italy: 1942-1945, A Personal Memoir. Max Corvo (Praeger Publishers, 1990)

ABOUT THE AUTHOR

America's entry into World War II presented Leon Weckstein with the need to become actively involved in the fighting. At the age of twenty-one he was anxious to rid the world of its tyrants and put an end to the uncertainty surrounding civilian life. In 1942, he made several attempts to enlist in the U.S. Navy but was rejected due to a mild astigmatism and the need for glasses. The recruiting officers suggested he go on a heavy diet of carrots and return in six months to try again.

As it did for every United States citizen under the age of forty-four, two months later a Selective Service summons arrived. Leon's draft number had been called and the U.S. Army wanted him to appear for active service—astigmatism, glasses and all. [The complete story of those early enlistment days and Leon's participation in the Italian Campaign can be read in his wartime biography, *Through My Eyes,* published by Hellgate Press in 1999.]

Placed on a duty roster when he reached Camp White, near Medford, Oregon, he was assigned as a clerk-typist in the head-quarters office of the 91st Infantry Division. But his fingers never touched a keyboard. Those first orders where promptly changed to do basic training as a private in the Intelligence and Recon-naissance platoon of the 1st Battalion, 363rd Regiment of the 91st Infantry Division.

During the months of infantry training and field maneuvers that followed, his regimental commander took note of the fact

Leon Weckstein receives the Legion of Merit
"...for exceptionally meritorious conduct in
the performance of outstanding services in
Italy from 4 July to 20 October 1944."

that, eyglasses or not, Leon had an uncommon ability to observe
targets of opportunity while manning the regiment's observation
post. Shortly afterward, Leon was given his corporal stripes and
within two months, earned the leadership of his platoon as the
1st Battalion's S2 Staff Sergeant.

The anti-Semitic needling he received during basic training
had diminished with the first few days of his actions at Italy's
battlefront, but Leon acknowledged that the ethnic implications
never completely left, prodding him to be the best forward ob-
server in his battalion. To press that point, he never missed a day
in the yearlong Italian Campaign, and quickly earned the respect
of his division's highest officers.

As the 1st Battalion's Intelligence Sergeant, his assignment
could not have been more suited to a long-felt need to strike

back at Hitler's avaricious militia. That desire was consummately fulfilled as he relentlessly directed artillery and mortar fire from diverse forward observation posts and often became the prime target of German forward artillery; an extremely dangerous business!

A host of foreign and American awards adorn the wall in his office. In addition to the usual they include the highly esteemed Legion of Merit; the Bronze Star; Italy's Cross of Valor; Poland's Bronze Cross of Merit with Swords; and Pisa's Silver Medallion.

At the time of completing *200,000 Heroes*, Leon Weckstein is ninety years old, in good health, and resides in Thousand Oaks, California, enjoying the pleasures he shares with his family.